▼ Make Mine a Double

make mine a

double

Why

Women

Like Us

Like to

Drink*

edited by

gina barreca

*Or Not.

University Press of New England

Hanover and London

University Press of New England | www.upne.com | © 2011 University
Press of New England | All rights reserved | Manufactured in the
United States of America | Designed by Eric M. Brooks | Typeset
in Whitman and Verlag by Passumpsic Publishing

University Press of New England is a member of the
Green Press Initiative. The paper used in this
book meets their minimum requirement
for recycled paper.

For permission to reproduce any of
the material in this book, contact
Permissions, University Press
of New England, One Court
Street, Suite 250,
Lebanon NH 03766;
or visit
www.upne.com

Library of
Congress
Cataloging-in-
Publication
Data appear
on the last
printed
page
of this
book.

5

4

3

2

1

Contents

▼ An Aperitif

*t*here I was, standing with a group of distinguished women at a Modern Language Association party a few years back, and I couldn't help but notice that our male colleagues all seemed to be holding martinis. It was quite a sight: two hundred men in blue blazers and tan trousers, all holding triangular glasses. Surveying the room, one of my colleagues wondered aloud why a man with a drink thinks he looks like Sean Connery from *Dr. No*, whereas a woman with a drink fears she looks like Elizabeth Taylor from *Who's Afraid of Virginia Woolf?* That said, she sipped her Chardonnay in silence.

Not one of us could come up with a snappy answer.

Why does the cultural cork pop when we put women together with the grape and grain? Why are there still raised eyebrows, pursed lips, and hand placed over the glass as if to signal "enough"?

For the most part, books about drink celebrate the social drinking of workingmen or guys in blue blazers. The titles for such books include words such as "jaunty," "urbane," and "beer pong." In contrast, the titles for books about women who drink include words like "depraved," "licentious," and "ignoring risks for the unborn child." Older whiskey and younger women still symbolize an accomplished man, whereas the iconic drinking woman is memorialized in Hogarth's engraving *Gin Lane*. Shamelessly inebriated, the drunken central figure helps herself to tobacco from a snuffbox, blissfully unaware that her baby is slipping over the staircase banister.

Women have been raised and praised to make decisions based on what's best for other people. Drinking—any amount—does not pair well with this mission of selflessness. *Gin Lane*'s wench, besotted by alcohol, neglects her doomed child. And so will we all, if we drink.

A woman is always teetering on the edge, about to fall into the abyss of self-indulgence. One glass too many—even just one glass—could push her right over.

We were taught to fear the loss of control that comes from too much drink. The seduction of liquor leads to other temptations, red and juicy like an apple, and it's a downhill spiral from there. Susan Campbell writes: "If I had been a drinker in high school, I would have gone home with the first guy who asked, borne three or four woods colts (that's what we called children born outside of wedlock then), and ended up for life in a trailer just outside of town. That's all from that first sip of Bud." We see how easy it is to go from a teen's first sip of beer to Elizabeth Taylor's drunken floozy Martha, a woman so fueled by drink that she humiliates her husband by sleeping with their guest—or worse, the soused mom of bastard children.

These—and so many other—cautionary tales about the woman who drinks always have unhappy endings. She ends up sad, fat, abandoned, and poor. Or she ends up debauched, her looks gone, her reputation and liver in equal shades of graying disintegration. Drunk, she is a bad wife and worse mother. The glue that cements the family, she herself has become unglued, and everything falls apart.

We were also taught to bear up, button up, and deny ourselves pleasure. We must master the art of self-denial and role modeling. We should live smug and petulant lives, the lives of those who merely inflict virtue on others. We should give ourselves up, like Joan of Arc to the flames, to our passion for abstinence.

Actually, Joan of Arc, the sainted warrior, was no teetotaler; in her diaries she records her taste for "sops," or bowls of bread soaked in wine. Perhaps the fear is this: if a woman is permitted happiness, she might also pursue delight—and what will happen to her if she becomes too accustomed to pleasure?

She might seek it on her own, without asking for permission or benediction. Since a woman ordering a drink is the quintessential embodiment of a woman pleasing nobody but herself, it's not surprising that she's potentially a pariah. A woman with corkscrew in hand is indulging an appetite with no benefit to anyone else; she's also vaguely threatening. She drinks the way a cat purrs, not to please or entertain others, but simply for her own satisfaction. I'm not talking about self-medication; I'm talking about pleasure. The difference between enjoying your cocktails and being a drunk is the difference between enjoying a nap and being narcoleptic. Some, though, find it easier to assume that such a distinction doesn't exist.

Curiously, it isn't only patrician men who uphold this argument. Pantaloon-clad temperance ladies who chanted things like, "Lips that touch liquor shall never touch mine!" were the precursors to the neoconservative antifeminists of today. They're the "preservers" of the ideals of "pure womanhood"—a figment of our cultural imagination contrived by a society that refuses to admit that many of its female members are actually human beings capable of making choices and acting in their own best interests. The Angel in the House, they insist, would no more sip a spritzer than she'd laugh out loud. These gatekeepers offer cold nonsense and keep emotion at arm's length, judging and preaching, refusing to accept that women's lives, like the lives of men, are often unsentimental and sometimes savage, filled with harsh circumstances, long nights, unreturned love, betrayal, bloodshed, and loss many times over, even if the women have gotten married, given birth, and followed the men's high standards of womanhood. These women cannot be thought to serve a strictly male agenda because, really, they are a breed apart. Somehow with drink, as with sex, it is supposed to be the woman's job to say "no, thank you, I'm not a bit interested" even—or especially—when she is. For too long, women have been encouraged to consider the denial of pleasure as an achievement.

The works gathered in this volume throw down a collective gauntlet to what I regard as a deeply scary cult of Nouveau Puritans who would police what women consume under the guise of "helping" them curb their own appetites. Apparently offering to safeguard women, what the cultists would actually like to do is place women in quarantine — but whether to protect them or to protect others from them is never quite clear.

Yet women have always managed to drink, often quite joyfully. Peasant women drink merrily in paintings by Breugel and van Dyck. Classy dames advertise French champagne. Victorian photographs show everyone from queens of England nursing their schnapps to Molly and Becky and Lily down at the Union Hall, throwing back beers with their fellow workers. By the 1920s, the flapper gets into the act. She cuts her hair, takes off forty-six pounds of undergarments and trades them for short silk skirts, goes dancing without a chaperone, and knocks down cocktails as if drinking were a spectator sport. Finally women were drinking spirits publicly, unapologetically, and with — to some — quite shocking pleasure. This "new woman" standing at the bar became a metaphor for a woman standing everywhere else she was not meant to be: the voting booth, the university library, the birth-control clinic.

That flapper at the bar was — and, I would argue, is — the embodiment of sedition. She upsets the system because she introduces something new into it. By giving an order rather than taking one, she creates a brief moment of cognitive dissonance. When a woman lifts a glass to her lips rather than serving libations to others (the acceptable and customary role of the barmaid), the world is both shaken and stirred. Unlike the woman behind the bar, who responds to the needs of others, the woman on a barstool demands to be served. She does not serve others. She is her own woman. She has become Mae West in *She Done Him Wrong*, Nora Charles in *The Thin Man*, Mrs. Robinson in *The Graduate*, and Samantha Jones in *Sex and the City*. With her first sip, she has broken a key taboo — what other trouble will she make?

▼ ▼ ▼

Drinking is never uncomplicated for women, especially for those of us who came of age during a time when we were encouraged to chip away at cultural taboos one ice cube at a time.[1] Nonetheless, many women discovered ways to enjoy drinking. Catherine Conant writes about how she loves "any gathering of friends and family where we can share good food and wines and tell great stories. The liquor we drink adds notes of grace and flavor to our rituals and relationships." Fay Weldon celebrates success and community with other writers around the world as she sat "by swimming pools in the Bahamas and sipped gin and tonic, sucked up cocktails with little umbrellas at the Moscow Writer's Union, enjoyed the best martinis and the best conversation ever in Hollywood, toasted Russian poets in vodka, Finnish writers in schnapps, and Australian publishers in Foster's." Amy Bloom invokes the historical reputation of the classiest drink of all: "Everyone from George Bernard Shaw to Napoleon to me says that champagne is the perfect drink. It matches your high spirits; it lifts your low ones. It offers comfort and a little irony in one glass, and it calls up the deep and irrepressible bubbles you have within you."

Yet perhaps Beth Jones most concisely sums up how we feel about drink: "Most of us have a complex relationship to alcohol. It feels good (until it feels bad), and many of us have alcoholics in our lives. We don't want our kids to drink until they can make responsible decisions. So it's a risk to write an essay about embracing the social, enjoyable, nonmoralistic side of drinking. But that's part of drinking, too: it's fun."

1. Thanks to the Ladies United for the Preservation of Endangered Cocktails, from whom I've adapted this phrase. In the words of the Ladies' website (lupec.org), the mission of the group is "dismantling the patriarchy one drink at a time."

Make Mine a Double challenges those who police what, when, and how women drink on the wrongheaded and sexist assumption that such policing is necessary to preserve familial and social order. In this collection, twenty-nine women — from many walks of life, and ranging in age from young adult to aging crone — talk about drink, offering newly blended perspectives on an old practice. Some toast the effects drink has on relationships with siblings, parents, children, colleagues, and lovers. Others write about drink and sex, drink and danger, drink and despair, drink and desire. Collectively and in conversation with one another, the essayists examine underlying and unspoken assumptions concerning women's lives that have been bottled up and sealed tight. They recognize drink as part of these lives. Underlying and unspoken assumptions uncorked have room to breathe.

Cheers!

GB

October 20, 2010

kristen dombek

▼ Speak-Easy

A Partial History of the War on Whiskey

t

1

he history of the emancipation of women in the United States is the history of a war on whiskey, waged through public shamings by means of prayer, hymn singing, stone throwing, and the demolition of saloons with everyday farm tools. It is the history of Carry A. Nation, saloon shatterer, mad bringer of "hatchetations" from God to Kansas. Instigator, in 1894, of a "petticoat riot" that ended with the sledgehammering of a stolen keg of whiskey on a Medicine Lodge street. Destroyer of the Carey Hotel in Wichita, where she not only took a cane to a Venetian mirror but ripped apart a nude painting of Cleopatra, because the problem of men's drinking and men's treatment of the bodies of women was, she felt, the same problem. Every description of her in the history books calls her "big": nearly six feet tall and 180 pounds, gray-haired when she became famous, with a fiercely lined, crumpled, angry face. In 1901, she found herself a hatchet, and from then on, when the Holy Spirit sent her a hatchetation, she would round up a group of righteous women and make a visit to a saloon. While they sang hymns and prayed, Carry A. Nation wreaked total havoc, splitting the bar like firewood and chopping the bar stools into pieces, shattering liquor bottles and glasses until the floor was soupy with splinters and shards.

In honor of this woman who wanted to end drinking in America, we should all, as I'm about to explain, raise a glass. In my case, this will be a Jameson, neat. Because the history of my emancipation is a history of whiskey, drunk by me.

1

2

This is not going to be about *Sex in the City* drinking—prettily dressed ladies worrying about men over sweet pink cocktails. It's not about the refined pleasure of the white wine spritzer by the pool, or the glass of Sauvignon Blanc before dinner, or the well-bought bottle of red parsed out in two-finger pours over the course of a three-hour conversation with a best friend. I practice each of these kinds of drinking with a fierce and grateful love. But what I had to get over, to live in the world, was paralytic, throat-clenching, soul-sinking shyness. So this is an essay about getting drunk. Sit on the same bar stool for ten hours drunk. Drink until the red-faced neighborhood Ukrainians start falling off their stools drunk. Accidentally go home with the bartender and then do it again the next weekend drunk. Maudlin weeping on the sidewalk drunk. Piss on the street drunk. And ride the subway home as the sun rises drunk. In other words, whiskey drunk. The kind of drinking that takes a hatchet to your sense of self, wrecks relationships, and kills people. Or if you're lucky, as I have been, that teaches you how to fall in love with the whole big world, and speak—albeit in a quiet, slurred voice.

3

Carry Nation was born in 1846 into a fervent fundamentalism in Garrard County, Kentucky, which now calls itself, in her honor, the "Birthplace of Prohibition." Born into chronic illness, by a mother so deranged she sometimes thought she was Queen Victoria. Grew to love and marry a Missouri man who was mean and died young of "the drink." Married again—to a man she did not love, or so the story goes, but with whom she made a life in Texas and later Kansas. All this time, something was brewing in her, as it were: a rage that would bring in a new century to the sound of shattered glass. Bar patrons and owners fought back. They threw stones and eggs and punches; they shouted nasty names. But this only encouraged her. By the dawn of the twentieth century, Carry Nation was famous, and it was time for her to take her show on the road.

4

This is the kind of shyness I'm talking about. The scene is an Indiana church lobby, in 1985. I am a skinny thirteen, with feathered brown hair, wearing a pastel flowered dress with an off-white pilgrim collar that my mother and I have sewn ourselves from a McCall's pattern. Across the lobby, Julie Shepard[1] is exiting the sanctuary with her family, every member of which has come to the evening service in khaki shorts. Julie's father looks exactly like Tom Selleck. Her mother has pale beige hair made of something like cotton candy, if cotton candy felt like finely spun clouds, and her ten-year-old little sister is like the cute funny little sister in a sitcom. Julie goes to public school and has highlights and a grown-up, pretty, round face. In the winter, her skin is creamy white, but she is currently (and every summer, all summer) very tan. She's got a kind of sly, shiny sweetness that makes her seem like an angelic cat, to me. We are the same age and have met in catechism class, where we memorize complicated theological answers to questions about what we believe. The normal thing to do, I can tell, would be to go right on over and talk to her. The problem is, whenever I get close enough to say anything — a distance which I am actually unsure about,[2] but whenever I do get within six feet of her, not to mention when I stand really close to her with our shoulders nearly touching while the fathers' Oxford shirts and the mothers' imitation Laura Ashley dresses eddy and clump around us — my head empties like a poured bucket.

1. Names have been changed.
2. And in fact I still am: at ten feet, can you be like, "Hey! Hello?" If the person you want to talk to is talking to someone else, it's weird for everyone if you approach from behind and kind of tap him or her on the shoulder. I've figured that much out. But if you're in front of the person and whoever he or she is talking to, and they would think it weird if you didn't say hi but the only way you can say hi is if you interrupt their conversation by saying, "Hey! How's it going!" — well, should you do it?

5

"Friendship with the world," wrote the apostle James to the early Christians, "is hatred toward God. Anyone who chooses to be a friend of the world becomes an enemy of God." I was born into a fervent Indiana fundamentalism, and my family took James's words to heart. We stayed home. Home school, home work (my mother taught piano in our living room, and my father didn't work at all). Homegrown food, in a garden that took whole days of tending all summer long. My brother and I weren't supposed to speak to adult visitors until spoken to, but there weren't many visitors. So we worked on quieting even our thoughts, at least the ones that were not spiritual but sinful, not godly but the kind of thoughts Satan or people from the world wanted us to have. It was that kind of place, my Indiana; it was them or us.

When Carry Nation went national, in those days before Oprah, she joined the Chautauqua lecture circuit, which happened to include the town that I grew up in, Winona Lake, Indiana. Like all Chautauqua sites, it had what was basically an elaborate summer camp and education center for Christians. But Winona Lake was more spectacular than most. It had a roller coaster that dipped and climaxed amid panoramas of biblical scenes. You could attend elaborate operatic pageants of Bible stories, the Old Testament ones complete with smoking altars. And you could attend self-help lectures on avoiding the temptations of the world, lectures by flamboyant speakers like William Jennings Bryan, the baseball player-turned-evangelist Billy Sunday, Will Rogers, and maybe even Carry Nation, who would have shouted and paced, hatchet in hand, and then posed for photographs with fans. In short, there was no need to seek secular entertainment. For a while there was even a wall around Winona Lake, and you had to pay to get in. The wall kept the world out, and the Christians in.

6

With her highlights and her public school sophistication, Julie Shepard seems worldly, even though she goes to church. She doesn't look like she really thinks about God that much, which is all I really do at this point in my life, and so I have trouble imaging what she does think about. But I am curious. And this Sunday, I'm ready. We drive an hour each way to get to a church that meets my father's particular theological specifications. In the car, I have spent my time trying to imagine what Julie Shepard's life might possibly be like, and what she might be interested in, and I have written down a list of things to say to her during the fifteen-minute period after church when everyone is supposed to talk to everyone else. And so now I walk over to Julie Shepard, and stand close — but not, I hope, too close — and ask:

1 Are there any shows on television that you like to watch? (We're don't have a television at my house, so after she answers, all I can say is "Oh," and there's a silence of almost a full minute before I pull myself together and try again.)
2 Do you feel that you can get as good a tan if you work out *while* you lay out? (Clearly, Julie Shepard lays out a lot, *and* works out a lot, so I think this is an incredibly clever question, but she just says, "You probably get a more even tan cause you're moving?" and I'm stuck again.)
3 You like khakis a lot, huh? (She looks down at her shorts and raises her eyebrows and nods).

And then I'm pinioned by silence, and a spot on the wall behind Julie Shepard kind of locks my eyes up and throws away the key. After a few minutes or hours, her parents call her and they sweep glamorously into their silver first-generation Ford Taurus station wagon, and my family lumbers into our hand-me-down two-toned Buick LeSabre, and we go off to our separate worlds.

7
By the time I came along, there wasn't much left of the Chautauqua circuit, except a couple of Christian conventions that continued to come to Winona Lake, which was in ruins at this point. But the spirit of Chautauqua remained. When I was

allowed to stop home schooling and go to high school, I went to a fundamentalist school where we obsessed over not having sex, not smoking, not drinking, not doing drugs. There was the occasional book burning, and the constant worry that non-Christians at the edges of town might be conjuring ghosts or demons, or just generally serving Satan somehow. As one of our chapel speakers demonstrated with a slide show, even liquor advertisements in magazines had subliminal messages written in the ice, about sex and Satan, similar to rock and roll lyrics when they're played backward. I spent a lot of time in the cafeteria bathroom, eating a sandwich from home, because I couldn't eat properly at the lunch table, where my strategy was to listen so enthusiastically to the conversation that no one would notice I wasn't talking. When I did try to eat in public, I couldn't eat properly. Once I sat across from Greg Coyle (who called me "Krystal" in the notes he passed to me in math class and who wanted to "go" with me), and he pointed out a big chunk of yellow Hostess cupcake icing on the sleeve of my navy ski jacket, which I then couldn't get off, no matter how many napkins I used. Greg Coyle stopped wanting to "go" with me after he found out how one-sided the conversations would have been, but I prayed for him because he seemed a little worldly. Actually I prayed for everyone, even the public school kids, whose high school was huge and had textured rubber floors like a space station. It was just on the edge of town, as was the Tippecanoe Dance Hall and every other frightening outpost of the encroaching outside world. I wished there were still a wall around the town. It felt like we were under siege.

I would have given anything to be like Carry Nation: a woman of certain and spontaneous action, of physical power, unafraid to speak my mind. But maybe I was really like her: I had a sharp need to protect myself by dividing everything into good and bad, right and wrong. The problem was that I, and everything I might potentially say, tended to end up in the category of bad, and wrong, and stupid (an extra-biblical category I'd added on my own). I know we breathed in the same air of absolute judgment,

Carry Nation and I, she in her Kentucky and me in my Indiana. I don't know if, as a child, she turned that judgment first on herself. But I recognize her particular rage. The anger that calls out for a hatchetation, that wants to splinter wood and shatter glass. Something like it was brewing in me.

8

Let's say that the authority that your father has over you is divinely ordained. ("Disobey me," my father was fond of saying, "and you disobey God." He liked to remind me that in Roman times, fathers could have their children executed for talking back.) Let's say you're not allowed to talk back to your husband, either. Same deal. Let's say you have become concerned about the widespread problem of drunken men beating and raping women and also dying on them. Let's say you aren't allowed to vote, and you are also not allowed to speak up in — or in some cases even enter — the very places where men decide these rules: the church, the town hall, and perhaps most important, the bar. What weapon do you have to wield? "You didn't give me the vote," Carry Nation liked to say, "so I had to use a rock." But of course the rocks and the hatchets were just theatrics. It's not hard to see how your best weapon turns out to be moral superiority, the ability to distinguish absolutely between what is good and what is bad for people. In this way a rage at drinking becomes a rage at silence, and a rage at silence find its voice in a bar. When Carry Nation made herself a vessel of God's hatchetations, she was wielding the very weapon that shut her up in the first place. They didn't give her the vote, so she had to use shame.

9

As a child, I loved Leviticus, with its elaborate rules for conducting sacrifices, building temples, and avoiding menstrual blood. Everything was laid out neatly: this or that, clean or unclean, now or then, ours or theirs. At my Christian college, I was delighted to sign a "Statement of Responsibilities" forbidding (among other things) lying, premarital sex, homosexuality, and pride. I pledged to "abstain from gambling, the illegal use of drugs, most forms of social dancing, and the use of tobacco and alcoholic beverages." But conversations didn't have those kinds of rules. At that college I felt so shy that I stayed mainly in my dorm room, under a soft pink blanket brought from home. Finally, I transferred to another Christian college, and there, I had my first real drink. It was gin, about a quart of it as I recall, all of which ended up on a beige shag carpet halfway up the flight of stairs to the bathroom at the off-campus house where my roommate's brother lived. I had not yet found my weapon, but I'd begun to hatchetate.

Here are some of the things I am grateful I did, from about age nineteen to twenty-three, which I never would have done if I had not then begun to drink thirstily and copiously, though not gin (never again gin) but whiskey:

1 Got into a lengthy contest which involved repeatedly jumping off the front porch of a house on campus into some shrubbery.
2 Threw a television out of the second-story window of the same house.
3 Drove very straight at exactly the speed limit down numerous streets in Winona Lake and Warsaw, Indiana, as well as Chicago, Grand Rapids, and New York City.
4 Had various members of the cast and crew of a certain regional theater try to get me to give them blow jobs, without any shame or embarrassment on my part for my total failure at giving said blow jobs, having absolutely no idea what the men were doing.
5 Danced in a long spiraling line with hundreds of people in a fountain in New Orleans while Dr. John and his band played "Walk on Gilded Splinters."
6 Stopped saving myself for marriage.
7 Dropped acid in a park full of thousands of people, having

bought it from a dealer named Astroshine without feeling afraid for even a moment.

8 Had — somewhere between the third or fourth drink and the blurry end of every night — thousands of hours of lubricated, avalanching, infatuated conversations with people I could suddenly talk to, and with whom I learned to relax enough to pay attention and say out loud, usually at an audible level, what came to mind.

I'm pretty sure I was hung over when I stopped believing in Jesus. One fall evening, somewhere in the middle of that list, I was sitting in my basement bedroom on campus, and the contradictions between all my beliefs (God loves everyone but God sends most people to hell, and so on) started to hurt so badly that I did something entirely new. I took a leap. I just stopped believing, and I fell into a world so messy that I'd never again find a set of rules to make it work by, though for years I would try. And in the moment after I stopped believing, I felt, for the first time, peace.

10

When I was twenty-four, I had an ex-boyfriend drive me to New York in a U-Haul I'd made him pay for. I broke up with him before the trip and again after it, once he'd helped me carry all my things up the three flights of stairs to my new apartment in Cobble Hill, Brooklyn. I would have done anything to get to the city. It was 1996. All that was left for me was the world I'd been warned about, and I needed a way in. In the first year, when I had few friends, my drink was still Jim Beam. On a Friday or Saturday night, I would buy a pint and head to the Promenade in Brooklyn Heights. I'd sit for hours alone on a bench there, listening to mixed tapes of the Pixies, the Grateful Dead, Joy Division, and Donovan, looking at the lights of Manhattan across the East River, and getting very drunk. Drunk enough to feel liquid, dissolved enough to sip the whole city into myself, and pour my own mind into the city, imagine losing and finding myself among eight million people. I was getting ready, but if New York City was the world, I was still on the outside, practicing.

11

Carry Nation died in 1911; in 1920, prohibition was signed into law. She and the women of the Women's Christian Temperance Union had successfully shamed an entire country. But like many women in the WCTU, Nation was angry about a lot more than drinking. She fought for suffrage, prison reform, and world peace, and against poverty. It is hard, now, to remember this, but before the Scopes trial and *Roe v. Wade* split our country's politics into their current camps, it was conservative evangelical women who fought for progressive causes — equal rights, civil rights, the protection of women from drunken physical and sexual abuse. Gospel causes, the kinds of things Jesus cared about.

As it turned out, Carry Nation and the temperance movement had created the conditions that would make it commonplace, and eventually legal, for women to drink in bars. Since the speak-easies were underground and illegal, all rules were off; for the first time, women who weren't sex workers drank openly and regularly alongside men. Perhaps it was not God but some angel of the future that sent Carry Nation her hatchetations. She walked into saloons to destroy them, but perhaps in some way that was secret even to herself, she walked in to say we should be here.

12

I found my first real home during my second year in New York, at a bar in the East Village. Maybe it was the kind of bar you've loved, if you've loved a bar. Down a few steps from the street, with a thick, worn wooden bar to the right, three booths with cracked brown vinyl seats to the left, a pool table in the back. Christmas lights coloring a firmament of smoke with red and blue and green. There was a bar that was its mirror image next door, but most people who went to my bar never went there. This was a whole world, and always enough.

The weekend bartenders, Edward and Paul, ruled the place. Edward was a character in his seventies, with thick, black-framed glasses and always dapperly dressed in vests and sometimes a cravat. He chain-smoked and made delicious whiskey sours, and because I was studying modern drama in graduate school, he always wanted to talk to me about Brecht or Kurt Weill, whom he had met, back in the day. Paul was a tall, long-haired bear of a man with an indefinitely incomplete PhD in English from Cornell and an obsession with all things Southern and country. He always knew more than anyone about everything but was terrified of, among very many other things, fire. So he had never smoked cigarettes, though he now tended bar in a place where most patrons had about five going at a time. I was perpetually broke, but when Edward and Paul were there, I always had enough to drink.

I usually went to this bar with my curly-haired friend Sarah, who had moved to New York from our college town that year, and who was giggly and wise, and perpetually falling in love with the patrons. We lived on the stools between the end of the bar and the window, where we could see everyone, and where Paul and Edward would lean, in between their trips down and back. I learned to talk in the few-minute increments that bartenders have for conversation: using short sentences, nothing deep, ready with a joke, ready to cut it short. I learned to talk to any kind of person who struck up a conversation with me. To be funny and not to care. A few Makers Marks and a Rolling Rock or two, and I was part of conversations that had been going on for decades among the old-time patrons and were now expanding to include the upstart East Village hipsters and everyone in between.

I had felt about Julie Shepard and countless others like a cat probably feels about another cat it's never met, looking at them sideways. But here, I faced people head-on. There was John, the red-faced Ukrainian alcoholic I talked to for hours about his train wreck of a life. The glamorous Ukrainian middle-aged couple, the man always in silvery sunglasses and the giggly blonde, who seemed to be somehow the picture of romance, who liked to watch each other flirt. Paul's circle of East Village punks and country musicians and artists. Muskrat, who would come in — always in a journalist's multi-pocketed khaki vest — and take a look at me and say uncannily accurate things like, "you've been going to the gym but you're still tired all the time" or, "you're getting a sore throat, huh?" and give me some kind of herb that would actually help. Muskrat, who was always coming back from New Orleans with voodoo potions, was evidently pretty much homeless but had put his two sons through Harvard or Yale (the sons were evidently dashingly handsome and came into the bar once or twice, but never when I was there). This was the world, finally. But as it turned out, it wasn't one world but as many as there were people to sit next to, as if what I had been scared of, on the other side of the wall, wasn't Satan, but how many different worlds — broken, partial, lovely, sad — there were to know, after all.

For a while, I spent probably twenty hours a week at this bar. I loved to come in during the afternoons, when the fading sunlight made curls of cigarette smoke look like fine, dancing spirits. Older Ukrainian men and a few women lined the bar then, and there would be a pool game or two going on, with the alternating pattern of quiet concentration, clinking balls, commentary, quiet. Mike, the owner, would come in at 6:00 or 8:00. He was a second-generation Ukrainian who lived a few doors down, an enthusiastic capitalist who was always trying to raise the bar's image, make some improvements. And then Paul and Edward would come in, and the night would really begin. The waiting for who would show up, and the news about who had showed up the night before. The slow spiraling conversation with whomever was there. Willie Nelson on the jukebox singing "Blue Eyes Crying in the Rain," *Sticky Fingers* and *Ziggy Stardust*, Merle Haggard and Elvis, Stevie Wonder's "Jesus Children of America," and always Johnny Cash. When the jukebox stopped, Paul would give Sarah and me dollar bills to feed it. If I got the hiccups, Edward would lay bitters and honey and lemon in front of me. If it was the first or second anniversary of my father's death and I was out on the steps, crying, Paul would bring me water. Every Halloween, he would decorate the place with fake spider webs, and all the regulars would pack in together in our costumes. Whatever night it was, sometime after midnight Sarah and I would dance in the narrow space between the bar and the booths, while Edward and Paul looked on and smiled. A couple of times, Mike or Edward got too drunk to work, and I'd get behind the bar, all the way inside now, making everyone else's drinks. The best thing was to stay until closing time, at 4:00 a.m., and then, after the door was locked, stay longer. To walk out into the next day's light, mindless and swervy, and go to Odessa for breakfast, and fall asleep, full of stories and music and whiskey, as the rest of the city woke.

13

Prohibition is back, at least in this city; the hottest bars are the ones you've never heard of, down a dark alley and through an unmarked door, or behind a secret sliding door at the back of a deli and down some stairs. You buzz to get in, and the servers may bring you your drink in a teacup or a paper bag. The ceilings are shiny tin, or the green of the ceiling of Grand Central station, the walls are wallpapered, the lights are low, and the drinks are complexly antique. Perhaps we're so free of Christianity's shadow that we're longing to fake the feeling of breaking rules in secret places. But look closely: the models are skinnier than flappers ever were, you can't smoke, and you'll find little of the exuberance of the old speak-easies. Everyone's watching everyone else. Everyone's watching herself: one drink a night, and don't touch the bread bowl. Do yoga long enough, and you'll start to hear about keeping your body pure. When I need to get a grip, now, I make lists of what I can and cannot eat. Organic is me, processed is them;

kale is me, steak is them. Nearly a hundred years after the temperance movement got its way, and far from any Kentucky or Indiana fundamentalism, we still divide good from bad and right from wrong; we are too often still masters of our own shame.

And we watch each other, looking sideways like cats, to see how we're doing. If you don't know what I mean, try getting pregnant. I've seen it happen to my friends dozens of times. Walk into a New York restaurant with a bellyful of baby, and your waitress will ask your tablemates for their drink orders, smile at you, and say, "Of course nothing for you!" You probably wouldn't dream of ordering a drink, but if you do, if you happen to hide your baby bump under the table and order a glass, or steal a sip from your friends, you're risking raised eyebrows or worse. Never mind that your mother probably birthed you with a martini in one hand and a cigarette in the other, and you turned out just fine. Everyone jokes about this, in fact, but the rule remains. Never mind that even a few minutes of research into fetal alcohol syndrome will show that it was invented in 1972 by doctors who, in their zeal for moral entrepreneurship (see the work of the sociologist Elizabeth Armstrong), ignored the scientific evidence that infant abnormalities are more contingent on social class, nutrition, and stage of a mother's alcoholism at the time of childbirth than on the amount that she was drinking during pregnancy, or even the fact that she was drinking at all. And never mind that you and all your friends would hit the roof if someone suggested you didn't have the right to end the primordial life in your personal baby incubator, for whatever reason you wanted. Your body, your choice — but you may not drink while you are pregnant, and you'd better be doing prenatal yoga, too. It's not about the new speak-easies, really, and it's not Carry Nation's fundamentalism, but prohibition is all the rage.

14

My East Village bar closed years ago. I had stopped going so much, anyway, distracted by a new boyfriend and a dissertation that evidently needed to be written sober, for the most part. I heard a while ago that John had died, and then Muskrat, a few years later. I'm angry at the drinking, if that's what killed them. Yet I wouldn't trade the hours I had with them for anything. Since the bar closed, I can't walk down the block where it used to be; I miss my friends, and that place, with a physical pain. I can still drink until morning, if I want to, but these days, I receive fewer and fewer hatchetations. I'm more likely to have the white wine spritzer, or two or four good fingers of Scotch. Fact is, what I learned to do by drinking happens all the time, now. I look at the strangers on the train, or the friends I'm having dinner with, or the students I'm teaching to write, and I start to get that whiskey feeling, that spread of warm joy at sheer, random life, as if the walls were yellow with age and the seats made of cracked brown vinyl, and smoke were curling like spirits in the afternoon light. I feel that sharpened inner listening, settle into the space between us, and say something, anything that comes to mind. And in the far booth, I can see her, the original hatchetator herself, avenger of women and drunks, a woman who split bars apart, so that we could, eventually, walk in. I raise a glass to Carry A. Nation, and she lifts her own, and winks.

▼ Just a Splash

"I'm sure you already know this, but the bar scenes are great." A guy in a creative writing class once scrawled this at the bottom of his tattered, stained-with-God-knows-what copy of my novel in progress. "I don't know why—I'm not implying anything—but maybe you should do more with that." Not implying what? Did he fear it would be indelicate to imply that I, a *girl*, a senior at Cornell, might have more than a passing acquaintance with bars? That I was writing about what I knew?

I was not offended. I knew he was right. I liked bars; I always had. Somewhere in my heart I still think that a paper umbrella perched jauntily atop one's drink is the height of glamour, and that music always sounds better on a jukebox. My parents had been shamelessly bringing my brother and me to bars ever since we were old enough to be propped up in highchairs; later I sought them out on my own, sometimes working in them. Before long, I abandoned that early novel, a fate it richly deserved. But the bar scenes had a life of their own; like ghosts, altered but recognizable, they kept returning, creeping stealthily into stories I wrote in later years. They crowded out nice subtle plots involving unrequited love and thwarted ambition, or drenched them in a smoky barroom haze. Eventually they demanded a book of their own, generating an entire collection of stories about a little girl growing up in—what else?—a bar. She sleeps in a little room beside the walk-in cooler, inherits old 45s from the jukebox. She lives on grilled cheese sandwiches, and she knows everything about everyone. This isn't grim social realism; it's a fantasy. She's more like a rustic Eloise than a victim of tawdry circumstance, if you ask me. It's an important distinction, too easy to miss.

Even now, as I work on a novel primly designed to avoid the all-too-familiar realm of seedy drinking establishments (see, that's not *all* I can write, I mentally point out to my long-ago critic, indignant), my characters keep popping into bars for a drink. *Just one*, they'll insist, and I sigh: I know what that means. They demand glasses of wine, dirty martinis, cold beers. I have no choice, it seems, but to write them into dim taverns, gleaming hotel bars, pulsing nightclubs; to stock their liquor cabinets and select lifestyle-appropriate stemware as though I were a desk-bound, pajama-clad personal shopper. I seem to have provided one of them with an elegant little flask, which is, frankly, the last thing she needs: better, after all, to stick to bars, to publicly sanctioned, communal drinking spaces; better to avoid stealth, above all. She'll have to ditch the flask, at some point. Bars offer more literary potential than solitary drinking, anyway: describe the smell in the air and name the song playing on the jukebox, and the joint comes to life; enter the bartender or a fellow patron, and you have a situation. *A girl walks into a bar* . . . It might be a joke, but more fundamentally, it's a plot. The possibilities are endless.

I do take their keys away when they've had too much, my errant heroines. I make sure they eat. I don't want them getting sloppy, messing up the story line. But I have finally resigned myself to the fact that I cannot keep them altogether sober. They won't have it. If there's a bar in town — and when isn't there? — they'll find it. And why not? I'm bound to torture them at some point: I'll doom them to loneliness or poverty, make all their loves unrequited, confine them to tiny hick towns in the middle of nowhere, dole out hope in anorexic doses. If they want to stop in for a drink along the way, I'm all for it; if they insist on another, I'll understand. If I'm feeling especially generous, I'll put Patsy Cline on the jukebox and give them someone interesting to talk to, someone who appreciates them.

I forgive my perceptive long-ago classmate for his suspicion that my accounts of bar culture did not spring magically from my writerly imagination, untainted by experience. But it is one thing to create more or less fictional characters and to act as a sort of godlike enabler and chronicler of their indulgences, all in the name of art, or something like it: they can slide off their bar stools, pass out in the woods, drive snowmobiles at night; they can live or die, agonize or prosper. In the end they have nothing to do with me. It is quite another matter to turn a clear, cold eye on the history — the legacy, even — that gave me the authority, all those years ago, to begin creating those characters. Is this a story worth telling? How far back must I go, I wonder, flipping idly through the darkened, crumbling pages of an old photograph album. I pause at my great- grandmother. Is that gaze sly, or defiant? Is she making a toast?

The first thing you notice about my great-grandmother in this picture is that she is wearing a sleek pantsuit with broad maroon and pumpkin stripes. It's bold. It's alarming. It's 1970. I am an infant; I am not in this picture, though I will appear a few pages later in an outfit shockingly similar to hers.

Next, you observe that she is raising a glass — a little tumbler, slightly askew in her outstretched hand, in which you can almost hear the ice clink. "Cheers!" she seems to be saying to the photographer, with a touch of obscure irony. Yes: that's the bit that needs explaining. I look long and hard at her. "Cheers!" is all she'll say. *Why should I explain anything?*

I don't really remember my great-grandmother, except in the delusional way that photographs make possible. What I do have, though, is a story. A drinking story, specifically; one that seems crafted to explain this very photograph. It involves a fiction of moderation. Grandmother would always swear, they say, that she'd had no more than one drink over the course of an evening. (Or maybe this is something that happened once, and as the story entered family lore, what had been an anomaly got recast as a habit, even a tradition.) "Just one!" she'd insist tipsily, implying a certain superiority to the more blatant sots in the room. But her claim was true, the story goes, only in the sense that she never permitted herself to see the bottom of her glass. A topping off here, a refresher there, a demure drop at intervals. A bottomless glass, never full and never empty. *Just a splash.*

I recently asked my father what Great-grandmother drank, and he seemed less certain than I had expected. Gin and tonics, maybe? Martinis? I do know that someone brought me a gin and tonic at a writer's conference last summer, when the other booze had run out. I took one sip and blurted, "It smells like my grandparents!" So let's say it's gin she's sipping, for the sake of continuity: Great-grandmother soon vanishes from the album, but gin and tonics do not. There on the lawn are my grandmother and my great aunt, sporting old-fashioned, skirted, floral bathing suits, passing my infant self back and forth and regarding me complacently over the rims of their cocktails. I gaze back, perhaps already learning to equate the sharp scent of gin and lime with the safety of being held in capable arms, the pleasure of recognizing admiration in the blue eyes fixed upon me, with the sun sinking over the river and casting long cedar shadows across sunwarmed skin. We all look happy.

In the following pages of the photo album, pretty young women with long straight hair, in multicolored tunics squirming with paisleys, lean over my brother and me — handing us toys, showing us how to wield tiny hammers, to tap rectangular blocks through rectangular openings, not the round ones. My mother and my aunt. Their hair falls forward, brushing our pale heads. They are always holding one arm behind them, though, keeping their drinks from sloshing on us, or preserving them, perhaps, from our curious, grasping hands.

As for me? Here I am: this picture is notorious in our family. It exposes me, unfortunately, as a greedy, furtive child. I am three, probably; my mother has taken the time to curl my long, still-fair hair, but the loose ringlets are already drooping. I'm wearing a stylish charcoal-gray dress with red trim and lace that

I swear I would wear now, if I had an adult-sized copy of it. It's a Christmas party, I think, which accounts for the box of fancy chocolates that rests alluringly on the coffee table I am sidling up to. Pretty chocolates, the kind that always look better than they taste—I can imagine the appeal; I can picture the delicate designs. My chubby hand creeps toward the table as if it has a life of its own, but my wary eyes are on the photographer. I know I've been caught.

This photo is amusing because it involves chocolate, of course—chocolate and a little blonde girl in a party dress. Chocolate is an acceptable, even charming, vice in women and children alike. But what no one has ever noticed about this picture, to the best of my knowledge, is what's next to the box of chocolates: a tall, sparkling glass of champagne, gleaming and golden, like some magic potion in a fairy tale.

Everyone has always assumed that I am reaching for the chocolate. I've studied the picture, examined the trajectory of my grasping little paw, analyzed the strategic position I've adopted in relation to the table.

And what I have to say is this: it is entirely possible that I am reaching for the champagne.

Frankly, I wouldn't be surprised.

Still in diapers but standing on his own, offering a stark contrast to my surreptitious holiday indulgence, my younger brother makes an appearance a few pages later. This isn't a holiday; it's a weekend night at home with spaghetti and cheap red wine, the air hazy with smoke and music you can almost see. He's decked out in a bright red shirt, a colorful, clunky wooden necklace, and someone else's large black boots. Note that I say nothing of pants. Clutching a wine bottle in his little hands, he grins brazenly at the camera. His plump cheeks, framed by cherubic golden locks, are flushed.

There's no subterfuge here, no secrecy, no shame. No sense of illicit complicity with the photographer. My brother is a miniature hippie hedonist, unapologetic and undisguisedly pleased with himself. I must be off to the side somewhere — or maybe I have trailed my mother to the kitchen, studying her disapproval; maybe I am learning what is illicit, and for whom. Maybe I am simply laughing, though. I seem to remember that we were all laughing.

Certainly there was plenty of drinking on the domestic front, in those years, but we also spent a lot of time in bars as children, my brother and I. We liked them. Yes, our parents drank. Too much, on occasion, no doubt about it. It has been suggested to me by several people — a teacher here and there, well-meaning friends, a guidance counselor, and finally a psychotherapist — that this was not ideal parental behavior. Perhaps there is something to that. But these days I wince if my friends and I stop in for a late bite at the pub downtown and I notice them casting judgmental glances at some wide-eyed youngster perched on a stool beside pint-sipping parents. Bad parents. Doomed child, surely. Suddenly it could be thirty years ago, and those glares could be directed at my parents, at me, happily doodling on cocktail napkins, sipping my Coke to make it last, knowing that the ice will melt eventually and I will end up drinking faintly brown sugar water, that I will pierce my maraschino cherry again and again with my straw in order to coax a little more flavor from it. "They're not hurting anyone," I want to say, "no one is getting hurt." But I don't. I am guiltily unwilling to give myself away, to proclaim a kind of solidarity with the apparently abused child.

I watch them, though, these children, and sometimes they watch me back; they are observant creatures. Frequently they are precociously well-behaved, and their big eyes brim with knowledge. "Not necessarily good knowledge," the prosecution will point out, but I'm not so sure: what kind of knowledge is bad? They look wise, the bar children. Occasionally, when I was small, well-meaning adults who were boozing in the same establishment as my parents would whisk me off (with my parents' reluctant permission) to spend the night with their unsuspecting children. They would plunk me down, pajamaless, in their living rooms and relegate me to the care of their baby sitters before returning to the cozy bar, no doubt congratulating themselves on having transplanted me to a more wholesome environment.

The baby sitters would paint their nails and talk to boys on the phone; I and my temporary friend would seek out the father's stash of pornography, or go through the mother's medicine cabinet; we'd watch horror movies on TV that provided nightmare fodder for years. I would think wistfully of the book I had left behind, and the quiet corner of the bar where I could be reading it, however unwholesome that corner might be. I was insufficiently grateful for such rescues, though some second sense told me that it was best to cooperate with these well-meaning gestures: my parents were frowned upon, I knew, for their penchant for what must have looked like dragging us along, for drinking in our presence, for failing to segregate the world of adults from the world of children.

I'm not suggesting that everyone pile the kids in the car and head on down to the local pub to get sloshed. But I will insist that I was not harmed by my exposure to even the seediest of establishments, or what I witnessed there; I wouldn't trade the habit of observation cultivated in the country bars of my childhood for all the baby sitters in the world. No one can convince me that tranquil domestic evenings around the TV would have prepared me more effectively for life. Give me the low, softening light, the unguarded laughter, the beer-fuelled storytelling of a bar any day.

So yes, the shadowy watering holes into which my unruly characters dart are, to some extent, resurrected from my memory. But my fictional women have a literary lineage, too: a legacy of semi-sodden, sordid glamour in which they seem determined to share, if only fleetingly. Lodged in my imagination alongside actual figures from my childhood are Jean Rhys's lovely, doomed, seen-better-days heroines, who sit in Parisian cafés sipping Pernods they can't afford, waiting for men who never come. Or F. Scott Fitzgerald's women, drinking desperately while their worlds crumble, not unlike his wife; or the title character of Daphne du Maurier's *Rebecca*, whose penchant for drink is one of her lesser vices, but still inextricable from her depravity and her beauty. Lushes all—like luscious, but less flattering. Consider the word: lush. Foliage can be lush, as can beautiful, densely patterned music. Flower gardens in which crowded, complicated blossoms compete for attention, flaunting vivid colors too strange and subtle to name, cloaked in dark and dizzying scents. Eyelashes that fascinate with a mere flicker, at least in movies. What is lush is lavish, luxuriant, profuse. It's extravagant, bordering on excessive. What is lush is often lovely.

Unless it's a noun, and then it's a drinker. A female drunk, and decidedly unlovely.

That voice again! Let's say instead that these women stake a claim for loveliness and invite us to join them. As for me, I like nothing better than to meet friends for a drink—a pretty cocktail, an overpriced glass of wine, a beer on tap. We have conversations over drinks that would be impossible anywhere else, I am convinced. You can revise yourself ever so slightly; you can tell your dreams. My characters insist upon it, and maybe that's why they keep ducking into bars.

More often, though, like my grandparents, we drink at home these days, out of the public eye, forgoing the seductively melancholy, communal cheer of the bar for smaller, more intimate gatherings at the houses of friends. Often I hold out my nearly-empty wine glass to a bottle-wielding host and hear myself saying, with stagy coyness, "Just a splash . . ." It's become a joke of sorts, my habit of saying this, and no one takes my apparent gesture toward moderation seriously: they laugh and pour generously, every time. But for me there are other layers of meaning to my words, private meanings, when I choose to acknowledge them. A nod, first, to my great-grandmother: "Cheers!" I never will know what she was thinking, but I can join her in her enigmatic toast. And then behind that another scene, fresher—half remembered, half imagined:

Not long ago, my mother, who had been ill, took a sudden turn for the worse and called me home. It was just before Christmas. I notified my brother and my father and boarded a flight. "It's like Mum's having a party," I wrote in my journal on the plane, still thinking of her deceptively lively voice on the phone. I knew it wasn't a party, not in the usual sense — far from it — but then again I couldn't shake the feeling: Mother was orchestrating a cocktail party to end all cocktail parties. Shortly after I arrived in my rental car to find everyone else assembled already, she confirmed my suspicion. "Want booze," she called from her chair, in an economical verbal shorthand designed to save breath, of which she had little, and produce a drink as swiftly as possible. My father's second wife ran to do her bidding and returned shortly with some fizzy concoction. Mother took a ceremonial sip and then allowed the glass to rest on the tray in front of her, her fingers loosely curled around it. Properly supplied with a drink, she looked around the room to make sure everyone was accounted for; satisfied that we were all in our places, she promptly dozed off. I kept an eye on the tumbler, now tilted sideways. It was a prop: with a drink in hand and her favorite people gathered around her, this was clearly a party — the last party she would ever have, which she knew perfectly well. Whether she actually consumed the drink made no difference at all, by then. It was the idea of the drink that mattered; it was the idea of the drink that transformed a gloomy vigil to the ultimate happy hour.

It was a triumphant bit of stage managing, I realize now. Cheers, Mum! Well done. In retrospect, I people the room with those unable to attend the celebration, for it was a celebration: aunts and grandmothers and great-grandmothers, heroines from novels, my past selves and my mother's. I let the crowded living room-turned-sickroom fade and admit in its stead the flatteringly dim light of the perfect barroom. Characters from my own fiction slip in unnoticed, settling themselves in the shadowy corners. The jukebox I leave to my mother; it's her party, after all.

But I think I hear, faintly at first, strains of Bob Dylan—nothing mournful, though, something you can dance to. Because people *are* dancing, suddenly—one of my heroines has begun it, knowing that stories demand some sort of action, hoping I'll let her stay. And I will; I'm in no hurry to let this moment end. "Cheers," I think, mentally raising my glass in a ghostly toast, and then holding it out for just another splash. *Cheers.*

▼ From **A**bsinthe to **Z**ima

An Incomplete Index

*a*bsinthe: You are twenty. Your hair is dirty but your eyes are bright, and you are studying abroad, have already perfected your ordering of a pint of cider, but then you read that quote by Oscar Wilde, the one about how drinking absinthe gives him the peculiar feeling of having tulips on his legs, so you slink from bar to bar in Prague whispering, "Absinthe, please." Most of the bartenders laugh, but then one gives you something and you suck down the licorice of it and palm your jeans waiting for blooms to explode from the holes. Outside, the sun sets twice; inside, you watch the bartender's mouth open and close like some kind of flower-turned-fish-turned-strangely sweet cannibal.

Beer: Also known as "the old standard." Invented in 9000 BC, discovered (by you) in 1986 (at the age of twelve, long before you'd even heard of the Czech Republic) when you were sneaking Pabst Blue Ribbons in the rec room. You took a sip, shuddered. Periodically, over the years, you think it's funny to drink a beer first thing in the morning. You watch as your mother or roommate or husband leaves for work (and your children for school), then you pop one open and turn on *The Today Show*. "Ahhh," you say, and swish the bubbles in your mouth.

Cosmopolitans: Or something equally girly and probably pink, inspired by a television show or particularly gorgeous weather and consumed in your early twenties or until you discover something stronger (see Martini). Every time you wrap your mouth around the word, you feel like a big old cliché, feel magazine slick and twice as empty, but still you say it. "Bartender," you say and keep saying until your knees are sour cherries and you try to find your way home.

Devil's Brew: The general term your grandmother, Mama Heaton—who, though surely driving a fine Cadillac in heaven by now, was an accused kidnapper and a devout sniffer of peach snuff—used for alcohol. "Nothing but the devil," she said. The term still haunts you, and on the mornings when your legs are decidedly not tulips and your mind spins so wildly that you've got nothing to believe in but God, you wonder if she was on to something.

Everclear: You are fifteen. Stacy Allen—still, even in your late thirties, the coolest person you have ever met—hands it to you in a Dixie cup. You sip; you puke; you vow to never touch the stuff again. Stacy holds your hair back and says you look pretty when you cry. You make note of this and spend the next twelve or so years trying to make yourself cry when you're around people you hope will find you pretty.

Fuzzy Navel: This is one of those slippery fish memories, but you're pretty sure it happened. You're almost certain, in fact, that from the ages of six to nine, during the 1980, '81, and '82 Miss America pageants (which crowned, respectively, Cheryl Prewitt, Susan Powell, and Elizabeth Ward Gracen, who later gained notoriety when it was revealed that while crowned she had what she called "unforced sex in a limousine" with then-governor Bill Clinton), you sat on the bed with your cousin and your aunt, and your aunt poured the three of you Fuzzy Navels—"Our secret," she called them—and the three of you sipped the peachy cocktails while eating not one but two containers of French Onion Dip and marveling at the slimness of the beauty queens' thighs.

Gin Fizz: A cocktail consumed by others. Men, probably. Or Europeans.

H-J: (see also pages 1–332); Hiccup of girl (11); hiccup of woman (16, 18, 23, 27, 29, 30–32, 35); hiccup of would-be (25), of has-been (27), of never-again (28, 37); peach hiccup (7); pony hiccup (25); Dixie cup hiccup (15); hiccup to end all hiccups (41); hiccup me, hiccup you (19); hiccup red, hiccup blue (34).

Kamikaze: You are twenty-four. After years of folding shirts in the mall and throwing bagels across a counter, you've finally landed your dream job: cocktail waitress. Your wrists are strong from carrying full trays of shots. Sometimes you think about the hot bartender you met in Prague; other times you think about the chef (those wings!) or some crazy Japanese pilots you saw on the History Channel. You wonder what it would be like to fling yourself into all that sky, to fly headfirst into anything at all.

Lemon Water: What Mama Heaton thinks you should be drinking instead. The glass should be sweaty; the front porch, hot.

Martini, Vodka, Up, Very Dry with a Twist (the "something stronger"): You are twenty-six. There are a thousand identities you're trying to rid yourself of. There's the little Jesus-loving Southern girl who wanted to be a beauty queen, and the wild-eyed beer-drunk girl with the hiccups. There's the wanna-be actress, wanna-be writer, wanna-be anything but a cocktail waitress shacking up with a mediocre chef (those damp crabcakes!). You're in the big city now; your legs *are* tulips! Walk into a bar. Sit on a stool, cross your legs. Keep your spine straight, for goodness sake, and say it: "Up. Very dry. With a twist." Just saying it will turn your past into a tiny, faraway star.

Navel, Fuzzy (see also Fuzzy Navel): When the past starts to get even fuzzier, you swirl peach schnapps in your mouth and will the memories to return to you, to travel through the deep empty space and find you, even though you've wandered so far away from home. And then one night, you go to another bar — or maybe it's the same bar but it's such a different night — and you sit down next to a guy from Missouri, only he turns out to be home. I mean, really, everything about him is home. Your hand in his hand is home; your leg on his leg. After a few hours, you walk inside him and pull the door shut.

O'Doul's: Also known as "the new standard," at least temporarily, as you've gone and gotten yourself knocked up. The man who was neither cannibal nor kamikaze, the one who found only marginal charm in your martini drinking, who taught you the bitters cure for hiccups, who listened soberly while you fleshed out your past; the one who years ago, in a dark bar, you called home—well, now he really is home (at least, both of your names are on the mortgage), and not only is he home, but there's also this: a baby, a baby growing inside of you, not a tulip or a fish but a girl, a tiny girl who will grow and grow and one day long to see Prague.

Pink Champagne: To be enjoyed at the many "mommy group" functions once baby arrives, preferably while nursing baby and discussing poop, sleep, or gender politics.

Qetiula (or to-kill-ya): But first, you are thirty-two. You've been dating a guy for a looooooooong time, a nice enough guy, a guy from Missouri, but I mean, come on, how long can you date? How old do you have to be before the word "boyfriend" feels like Reddi-Wip spewing from your mouth? Get on a plane and fly with your best girlfriends to Austin. Order a shot of tequila. Drink it. If you can still spell tequila, order another one. Repeat until your legs are worms.

Rum and Anything: And then, you are thirty-three. You've been dating a guy for a looooooooong time, a nice enough guy, a guy from Missouri, but I mean, come on, how long can you date? How old do you have to be before the word "boyfriend" feels like Reddi-Wip spewing from your mouth? Get on a plane and fly with your best girlfriends to somewhere tropical. Order a drink with rum. Slug it. If you can still say "rum" without shaking fake maracas, order another one. Repeat until your legs are blue sky.

Sweet Tea: Mama Heaton's sole alternative to lemon water. It seems like every summer day of your childhood, she sipped it and told you to be careful what you wished for.

Uh-oh: You are thirty-five. And (Whoa, Nelly! Holy crap!) you wake up and you got it! You got what you wished for: you're married! Not only are you married but you've got a baby and she's crying in the other room. Most days it all feels good and right, and you love them so much you want to devour them both, consume them completely — but then there are the moments (the noise!) when your heart spins off its axis and you start thinking about how you should be in Paris or Prague, taking lovers and writing poems and eating *moules frites*, and "Oh," your lovers would say in a room so quiet, "your legs are as smooth as — " and you'd hold your hand over their mouths so as not to let the sound escape, but it would come out anyway. "Tulips," they'd say. "As smooth as tulips."

Whiskey: But you don't make it to Prague because you're still nursing and don't want to carry the pump, and you're trying for No. 2, heck, maybe you're even trying for No. 3, so you find yourself at a poetry reading — because you suddenly remember YOU'RE A WRITER!!! YOU READ OSCAR WILDE!!! YOU DRINK SCOTCH NEAT!!! — and the playwright, the one who's up for at least a Pulitzer, has got his hand on your thigh, and you're pretty sure he can feel your Spanx but you don't care because he's just ordered two more drinks from the cocktail waitress, and, "Your eyes are hypnotizing," he says.

Xx: Only the next morning your eyes are anything but hypnotizing. They are two Xs scraped (as with a yard tool) into your aching skull. Your daughter has a fever, you are a wreck, and your husband is pressing a cold compress to her head then your head then her head again. You ask him if you can all move to Istanbul or Kansas City or anywhere at all. You make secret promises to God about how you'll never drink again, but that night at dinner you let your husband pour you a half a glass of Shiraz, and you keep telling him how sorry you are, how sorry you are that you were sick, how grateful you are to be home. You cry and think of what Stacy Allen told you in tenth grade. Every twenty minutes or so, you go to your daughter and make sure she's cool to the touch.

Yellow: It's her favorite color. (Your son prefers blue.) She is a whole garden of a girl, and you want her to know everything about the world. But perhaps more than wanting her to know everything, you want her to know nothing. It is summer. She sits between your legs, and you brush her hair back and try to smooth out the lumps in her ponytail. You take a sip of your white wine spritzer (almost golden under the spell of the sun). She spins. A kiss. "I love you, mama."

Z at last: Summer after summer comes. You visit Geneva, Tokyo, Rio. You are a family, a happy family, light-years away from the dirty gingham curtains of Mama Heaton's kitchen. When you look out the window, you don't see a beat-up station wagon and an old dead pecan tree; instead, you see the wings of the plane and the bright side of the clouds. Way up there, so close to the kamikaze blue, you believe that if you show your daughter enough of the world she won't have to want anything; if you give her a little bit of everything, you reason, you'll somehow relieve her of unnecessary desire.

But, of course, the plane will land. It has to. You'll take the long drive home, surprised by how green everything is this time of year, and then some late afternoon when you're down in the kitchen, staring at a blinking cursor and sipping on something terribly refreshing, you'll hear noise coming from the rec room, and you'll go to see what all the fuss is. Your daughter, twelve, will be sipping what you recognize as a Zima; her friends — their smooth white teeth shiny and new — will be laughing. You shudder (first) at her bad taste and then again; your legs wilt; you pull the door shut. Later, you'll ask her what she did with the girls all afternoon, and when she says, "Nothing," you'll brush her hair — already getting darker with age — away from her eyes and marvel at the secrets we bottle up in our hearts, how early they start, how long they survive.

▼ This American Martini

t
Act One: Preface — The City
his small, postindustrial American city is block after block
of beer, sports stadiums, and the grunt and sacrifice of workers.
Each enclave of the city reveals itself only slightly when pressed
against. Deceptive wooden door, heavy and creaking; palms of
strangers' hands flat and firm against its metal plate; a darkened
room. Lining the entire right wall of the room, a long mahogany
bar; behind the bar its keeper, casually awaiting a customer (in
this version, the sun has not yet gone down, though it is cloudy;
the workers have not yet been released). In the corner of the
darkened room, a television; on the television, a game or a race
or a match. Draft beer pulleys abound, about twenty of them
with as many brands in bottles. There are three kinds of vodka,
and I am grateful for the choice.

As a martini drinker in the postindustrial city, I've become
peculiar and picky — some might say an annoying snob, others
might say a pretentious grump. In my own defense, it's not as
if the things I desire to make my life a little more satisfactory
are of an other-worldly order. A barroom sans oppressive artifi-
cial light. A group of close friends who all share a biting ironic
sense of humor; the exhilaration of making art; and a perfectly
prepared, transformative martini. Since encountering the postindustrial city, I've left those friends in my last city and find myself a fish among the earnest. I'm often forced by profession or
social engagement to endure a room swathed in throat-cutting
brightness (and not from a window). And, on the days I am lucky
enough to peel my head up from the concrete floor of ennui, I
am usually not lucky enough to write any poetry, or make any

art, but instead muddle around waiting for summer when everything including my heart convexes and gets gleaming again. In short, I put a lot of eggs in that martini basket, so when the martini arrives gray from too much olive brine, or coppery from too much vermouth, or — God forbid — lukewarm, I send it back. If the martini is wrong, everything is wrong.

I prefer vodka martinis to gin and like them served "up," when the liquor kisses the lip of the glass and I must kiss the lip of the glass and sip before making any attempt to transport it. There's nothing practical about the martini. Instead, the martini is an exemplar of excess, something you surely don't need but luxuriate in anyway. You can't drink martinis all night, or you're drunk before dinner and massaging the knee of the person sitting next to you, not your lover, who is, of course, on your other side. Martinis require a thing I do not have — restraint — but I love them anyway. A martini "up" must be served in a special glass shaped like an upside down triangle, what might be called a V; even if the glass is not rim full, walking with a martini is not easy. One cannot gesture wildly while talking. The body must be held a little tighter, which is why I suspect New Englanders, or at least people from upper-crust Connecticut as I imagine them, have a preference for martinis as they reinforce an already ingrained social code of the body. When holding a martini, one is required to take measured steps and pull the elbow in toward the body so that the arm, if moving, is anchored by the connection between the elbow and the side. Martinis can femme up the butchest girl and make the most macho guy appear a tad fey. The martini, in other words, is intentional, transformational. You think you're in control of it, but really the martini is a disciplinary apparatus, dictating not only the body's movements, but inescapably one's sense of self before the first sip is taken, and the nature of one's awareness afterward. The martini trains the body. Its normative "effects" or whatever are disrupted in the holding of the glass, the sip–long break–sip rhythm, the good taste of the whole performative affair. Without much effort, then, the martini can pull us, however briefly, from our burdened class roots. Unless you're doing it all wrong (chugging falls into this category; so does abundant spilling), the body is immediately trained toward some other "higher" articulation.

I'll say now that I mention the postindustrial city, the stadiums, and the beer because, as fate would have it, I've ended up living (temporarily at the very least) in a city that is everything I've been running away from — desperate, red-eyed bodies on street corners, sharp I-fucking-dare-you-to-look-this-way stares into passing car windows, fragile souls breaking inside themselves and over others, and a casual "it is what it is–ness" to the seemingly timeless package. To be fair, this postindustrial city, the one I live in now, has a striking beauty to it. You approach downtown from the airport via a tunnel carved through what I assume to be a mountain. Here the city announces both a confident yearning and a John Carver-y sense of possibility. We see the thing itself, the shimmering city open to us with its fountains and history, rivers and promise, the color of activity, and bend after bend of bridges from one thing to another. The city wants something; it desires; it reaches for another life. What the city lacks now, perhaps, is embodied in the martini — a contrived sophistication so entirely altering that one can rethink the self. The martini does not want. The martini simply is.

Act Two: A Visit "Home"

If there are ghosts, and there are, they do not present themselves but instead linger within white walls, blending, so that the haunted is uncertain of their presence. On the burgundy leather sofa in my mother's living room, a flash of an imagined child — me, swinging on the living room door as if flying; a scent memory, unpleasant and grimy; a rapid series of images, each as still as death. I have arrived five hours late for a forty-eight-hour visit after having driven on a wildly detouring route, lingering at a shopping mall, and purchasing a pint of Absolut vodka and a small jar of Spanish olives. When I finally arrive, my mother and I fall into our usual dynamic. We are stereotypes. We wrestle with one another in one of those typically fraught mother-daughter relationships; it seems beyond us, and yet is us — and only us — in action. My mother insists on thing after thing, idea after idea, and I attempt to resist my usual trajectory in which I devolve into a person locked inside a precise, haunting, tangible anger. Resistance, in this instance, looks a lot like the thing itself. When one clenches the jaw in resistance, the jaw is clenched, isn't it? In a blue plastic cup, then, I mix a secret dirty martini, so dry that the vermouth is still at the liquor store on a dusty shelf.

I should say here that the problem is not my mother, who is elderly or almost elderly now. (I noticed on this trip with an intake of breath that the shape of my mother's mouth in relation to her teeth is changing. I've seen this exact alteration of features on other older people, most prominently on my father, whose two-year-long death from a cancer of the blood aged him rapidly and dramatically, so that as he lay in the hospital bed on the last day I saw him alive, he seemed like someone flaccid and adrift, perhaps related to a person I once knew.) My mother and I, after all, love each other. My anger, then, while sometimes misdirected at my mother or the house or my deadbeat, jobless twenty-five-year-old cousin who happens to currently live with my mother, is really about the "situation." My therapist would call my stealthy martini "self-medication," but that's only because she relies on the prepackaged language of psychoanalysis to describe everything. The Bright Eyes sing into my headphones, "Let the poets cry themselves to sleep," and there is a bit of that too this night, but also a saving grace, as when you discover that the green algae that is the essential element of your diet is also a medicinal herb that clears the head and lets you descend back into your lost body.

A light-year is a unit of distance. How far away are the stars? How far away is the next galaxy? A single light-year is equal to approximately 5,878,630,000,000 miles. I am a light-year away, off in another galaxy. Drama of the room, its fifty-foot ceilings draped in translucent Egyptian white scrim, its massive white columns and white upholstered sofas, subtle lighting, a prominent twinkling walk out to the infinity swimming pool, pool beds and canopies, swaying palm trees, lush tropical gardens. My martini tonight is a cosmopolitan, flecks of ice floating on the surface. I take a long sip. My girlfriends and I have come because spring is near, but winter still has the Northeast in its brutal grip. We have come to fill our bodies with sunlight and awe. Bottle service is encouraged, but we sink into the beds with our feet resting on the pool's edge and order one cocktail and then another. Suddenly, we are these women, away in early March basking in the forever Miami sun, and everything is possible.

In my mother's view, a good Christian does not drink (I am actually not a Christian, not religious at all, but that has no effect on this line of reasoning). Anything other than "a swallow" is ungodly, sinful, ugly. A good Christian woman takes care of others instead of herself. If one is bending over from firewater, one is much less likely to bake a ham. My father, in contrast to my mother, drank — and did so, I believe, to survive. Until he retired at whatever age, he worked two full-time jobs. That means that Monday through Friday he worked a 7:00 a.m. to 3:00 p.m. shift and a 4:00 p.m. to midnight shift, arriving home — long after we were all securely tucked in, well-fed, warm, and rubbing our sleeping bellies — to eat his dinner, which was heat-congealed in the oven, alone at the dining-room table. Sometimes I would find him there in the half-glow from the kitchen, eating quietly in the near-dark, the clack-clack of the fork against the plate and a mouth full of false teeth, and wonder how any of this was possible.

Although the house itself haunts, the neighborhood of my childhood feels almost entirely foreign to me now. When I visit these days, when the weather is nice, I bring my bike along and ride around the places where I rode my bike as a kid: the high school, the mini strip mall, the corner candy store, another mini strip mall. None of it seems familiar; no sentiment or nostalgia nudges into me. I have the memory of being here, but it's as if that memory comes through a jar, all the edges rounded, the events themselves obscured and strange. My mother tells me of a cousin here who, although forty-six and able-bodied and male, "does nothing"; another who is recently released from prison; another who is "crazy." What's wrong with the crazy one, I ask. "I don't know," she says. "Does her mother know?" I ask. "I've never asked her," says my mother. My mother's good friend, whom I remember vaguely from childhood as being "scary," has a son in his forties who ignored his diabetes until he developed gangrene and had to have his leg cut off below the knee. He's on disability now, so he also "does nothing." "Maybe he wanted to die," I say. When I say this, I might as well be holding a second blue plastic martini. I believe, in fact, that I am. I wonder how this neighborhood, which seemed safe and "normal" to me when I was a kid, could produce such heartbreaking misfits. I'll tell you a secret. I'm afraid that I'll be left to occupy for a long time this hole that fragmentation has dug, this operation on site with rusted tools — that one day, perhaps, I won't be spending a Saturday afternoon on a blanket in Central Park reading the *New York Times* or at the Waldorf Astoria's Bull and Bear, smoking a cigar (it used to be a cigar bar, but now it's a steakhouse) and having a single, massive $25 martini with my girlfriends but instead "doing nothing" in a manner where my leg is disposed of in a medical waste bucket.

Act Three: The Most Popular Girl in School

"Careful," my plastic martini whispers in my ear, "you don't want to become a bitter woman. There's nothing less pretty than a bitter woman." I take another sip, nodding silently. "This is not what I meant," I want to tell the martini, "this is not the story I want to write." The martini shakes its head, disparagingly. "If I weren't writing about drinking martinis," I reply, "I'd be drinking scotch right now, the strong silent type, instead of being forced to endure the whip of your sarcasm." My martini performs a gesture that's akin to rolling its eyes; I guess I should say it turns its olives. "Whatever," it mumbles. I get the sense that it has a certain disdain for me, that it is looking down the long stem of its nose, shall we say. But I don't care. I realize that the martini is the celebrity. I'm the star fucker. I'll ride sidecar, do all the behind-the-scenes grunt work, what have you. The martini is an untrustworthy companion, but I'll take the risk.

I am sitting in a red restaurant in Northampton, Massachusetts, with a sort of date. We're both drinking martinis. When the conversation stalls, I glimpse a face I think I know at another table. She sees me, recognizes me, and poof, she is at our table — the iconic most-popular girl, or MPG, from high school. I'll call her M. M was a virgin and a bad girl, a Christian yet depraved, cute but not gorgeous. She achieved mythic status, however, only after our sophomore year, when her parents sent her to a high school for mentally ill youth. Being gone and "crazy" made us worship her more. I hadn't seen her since we all got word of her institutionalization, but there she was, right in front of me like the second coming of Christ. A miracle. I gasped. M here in the flesh, sipping, I noticed, white wine in the dead of winter like a dodo. I am holding my little celebrity in my right hand, taking a sip, then chatting casually, when M says, "I don't remember you being so sophisticated." "That was a long time ago, wasn't it?" I say. I was wearing Emporio Armani tuxedo pants (bought on sale at 80 percent off, but who cares?) and a black T-shirt, but it was the martini that winked (as it is wont to do) and sparkled like a time before our time, with a certain — yes, MPG M — sophistication.

As a class climber raised in the maw of urban decay (see Act Two), the martini adds to my cachet, helps me build my cult of personality and beat back the crunching persistence of past lives (see Acts One and Two). I suppose my love of the martini occurred by happenstance, that I simply stumbled upon the martini during my first stint in graduate school, muttered, "hello, old friend," and off we went on a wild excursion together. It isn't really possible to escape the network of constructed blacknesses projected into the consciousnesses of the American populace writ large, but I can pretend, can't I? I don't recall a single Hollywood movie in which a black person is drinking a martini. I do not mean to claim that there are no popular cultural productions in which a black person is drinking a martini; there probably are. But if the *Family Feud* category is "alcoholic drinks that black people drink," the martini is surely low on the list. The closest the viewer gets in the black-and-white films of the 1930s, when martinis were the height of cool and worldly wisdom, is a tuxedoed black hand reaching to serve one.

Despite MPG M's youth crises and subsequent stint at the school-hospital, I would never have imagined a burnt-out fire years later when we're both adults. The day of our chance encounter, I saw a vacancy behind her eyes, a thoughtful nowhere or everywhere, I'm not sure which. Whatever it was, her gaze didn't catch me in its hold the way it used to do for all of us who were wrapped up into her experience. Maybe I didn't need her as much. After all, I had my martini. M and I were friends, I guess, though back in high school she seemed more akin to what my martini is now: a celebrity who let me hang around. M sent me one letter from the school-hospital shortly after her arrival. She had rubber-stamped it several times, as if in a fever, with a mad, hair-shocked face. They can't bring this girl down, I'm sure I thought then, she's laughing all the way to Saint-Tropez.

Act Four: Epilogue

The martini — more its symbolism of carefree privilege than its potent delivery of intoxication — has helped me write my way out of one story and into the one I imagined for M all those years ago. Is the martini really transformative? Beyond its ability to get one really drunk, probably not. It belies a certain awareness, and even though it can discipline the body into certain movements and behaviors, that discipline is fleeting. The body gets soft, the martini spills anyway, and all self-discipline goes out the window (see the moment in Act One about massaging the knee of the person sitting next to you). We cannot, then, rely on the martini as an agent in our own transformation. But symbolically, the martini offers us something on the other side of yearning, access to an interiority free from impurities and where we are defiantly ourselves. Enter the dead. They bang noisily on a glass partition. I stare at them, then turn my back to the glass.

In the postindustrial city, secluded from the twittering hubbub of the university, vaguely lulled by the televised hum of a sports announcer, and in the relative quiet of a cave-like bar, as I resist most of my tendencies toward snobbery and simply choose a vodka for my martini — Stolichnaya — I feel a bit like the only survivor of a smoking train wreck. Strangely upright, I brush off my soot-drenched clothes and look around, saying out loud in a panicked voice to no one, "Damn, I'm lucky." It happens that I'm standing dangerously close to the train, not moving or feeling threatened, and we're in the middle of a ghostly nowhere, no house or road in sight, and I seem to have misplaced my cellphone. In my right hand is a broken martini glass, but a big sip miraculously remains at the bottom, along with one fat olive, and somehow I can't resist drinking it, glass fragments be damned. "Here's to everything!" I toast. The barkeep got it just right.

▼ Against Mixology

When I walk into a SoHo gallery, I expect to be snubbed. One look at my shoe-handbag combo, and even the intern knows I can't afford the art. At an alt rock show in Williamsburg, I am game for shame at the door. I'm not that young anymore, and all my piercings are hidden. Basically, if art is on the line, I'm okay with elitism.

When it's a question of sin, however—and no matter how much we dress up drinking or call it by a fancy name, it remains just that—judgment is absurd. People want their sin the way they want it. This is something every drug dealer and pornographer knows, so why can't today's upscale bartenders understand? To the so-called mixologists, I say: Pour up and shut up.

The problems with mixology begin with the word itself: a clumsy cocktail of Latinate root and Greek suffix appropriated by a lunatic fringe within the bartending world. The word offends the ear and seems acceptable only after repetition. In fact, I'm sorry I've already used it so much; the healthy contempt you felt when you first read it is probably fading, just as an unpleasant odor will go away if you smell it long enough.

In his 1948 essay "The Vocabulary of the Drinking Chamber," H. L. Mencken called the word "silly" and cited it as evidence of bartenders' "meager neologistic powers." It's kind of sad to read this Mencken essay now. He obviously expected the word to die the quiet death it deserved, but for once in his life he was too optimistic. Not only did it survive, it bred. Modern drinking chambers resound with pretentious neologisms; if you want to learn some, just pick up an issue of *Imbibe* magazine.

41

"Edible cocktail" and "solid" are two of my favorites—both mean "Jell-O shot."

The insidious thing about words is that the act of decrying them promotes their usage. Mencken did just that: *Merriam-Webster's Collegiate Dictionary* gives 1948 as the date of the first written use of "mixology."

If you have never encountered a mixologist in the wild, consider yourself blessed. Maybe you live in a nice college town where people still smile at each other in the streets. You patronize a clean, well-lighted place where someone called a bartender smiles, prepares your favorite beverage, and lets you drink in peace.

Enjoy it while you can. One gray happy hour you will go to your clean, well-lighted place to find the windows boarded up, the address obscured by a skull and crossbones, and the name of the establishment changed to something like The Pharmacist's Revenge. The horrible, sinking feeling in your stomach is called mixology.

If you are thirsty enough, go inside. (I know it looks closed, but that's just a trick to scare off customers.) Once your eyes adjust to the crepuscular gloom, you will be menaced by a beautiful hostess. Remain calm; you have every right to be there. Don't let on how badly you want a drink, but act bored. This should be easy if you listen to the music being played now that the cool jukebox has been replaced by the mixologist's iPod.

You may now proceed slowly toward the bar, which is the large object in front of you made of zinc or tin, groaning beneath the weight of all the fruit infusions. Behind it stands the man whose sole purpose in life is to keep you from your drug of choice. He is probably a white male in his late twenties with a handlebar moustache, mutton chops, or pubo-Amish beard. He dresses like a member of a barbershop quartet. A frown hovers on his face as he surveys his vast collection of bitters.

The worst mistake you could make at this point would be to wave a twenty. This will offend the mixologist's dignity. Like a cat, the mixologist must acknowledge you in his own time, if he does so at all. Don't snap his suspenders; he bites.

That jewel-encrusted, leather-bound volume he is sliding in front of you is not *The Complete Works of Shakespeare* but the *Seasonal Cocktail Menu*. You now have two options. You can flip past the prologue about the good old days, when men were men and India was a colony, and scan the list in search of something that doesn't contain truffle foam, tarragon caviar, or housemade miso bitters. Or you can bravely close the menu and say, "This looks amazing, but I think I'll stick with my usual." Depending on what the usual is, be prepared for some humiliation.

The last time my dad came to visit, shortly before he died, I took him to Smith and Mills, a tiny bar in Tribeca built of reclaimed industrial fixtures. As a city planner, Dad was sensitive to the beauty of architecture, and I thought he'd like the quality of the space.

In his broad Oklahoman accent, he ordered an Amaretto sour.

I'll never forget the way the waiter smirked. "We don't serve those here."

"Why not?" Dad asked.

"The mixologist doesn't like Amaretto."

My father looked hurt and confused. He was probably trying to simultaneously parse the word "mixologist" and understand why it mattered whether *he* liked Amaretto, since it was my *father* who was going to drink it.

"Do you maybe want a whiskey sour, Dad?" I asked. "They're really good here."

He shook his head stubbornly. "How about a *mojito*?"

This time the waiter actually laughed. "We don't have those this time of year."

I forget what Dad ended up drinking. Whatever it was, the mood had been ruined. He felt like a hick, and I felt like a jerk for exposing him to such unkindness. This was an ongoing theme in our relationship. You can never make up for a childhood spent apart, and Dad and I were always out of step in each other's world. We were always thirsty for something that wasn't on the menu. A bar should be the kind of place that lubricates such tensions, rather than aggravating them.

Maybe your usual is something more chic than my father's, though, something irreproachable like a Manhattan. I can assure you that a top mixologist will still find a way to put you in your place.

The frown will deepen above the Amish beard as he shaves ice off an enormous block and piles it into a cocktail shaker. He will fire off a rapid series of questions, ostensibly to tailor the drink to your taste. Don't be fooled; every question has a very clear right and wrong answer.

"Rocks or up?"

"Up, please."

"Perfect or sweet?"

"Um . . . perfect, I guess."

"Shaken or stirred?"

"Stirred?" Good answer! It's considered terribly un-Mixologically Correct to shake a Manhattan.

"Angostura bitters or housemade miso bitters?"

"Angostura."

"Cherry or twist?"

"Twist?" Correct again! This particular mixologist has authored a series of scathing blog posts denouncing the cherry garnish.

"Rye or bourbon?"

"Uh . . ."

It's not your fault. You are tired and thirsty, and from up close that beard is really scary. You say something disastrously un-MC: "I'll take Maker's Mark."

The mixologist's face relaxes. He strokes his ascot with a little smile. "We don't carry industrial liquor here."

"Industrial?"

"Any brand that has a production of over a thousand cases a year."

"Oh."

"In addition, most educated drinkers agree that rye whiskey gives more complexity to the finished cocktail than bourbon. Since you're obviously a little new to all this, let's start you off with a Kentucky rye that's been aged in Madeira cask and contains thirty percent corn . . ."

Try to stay perfectly still and say nothing, like an animal playing dead. Hopefully his lecture won't last longer than twenty minutes, and you'll get your drink at the end. It won't be as good as your usual because it will have way too much bitters and will cost twice as much. But you'd consume paint thinner at this point just to shut him up.

Don't get me wrong: I'm in favor of the well-made cocktail, and I love serious bartenders who take pride in their craft. The gin martini is the official alcoholic beverage of my marriage, and the world would be a better place if every bartender knew how to make one. My husband, a touring jazz musician, drinks them wherever he goes "very dry, stirred, with a twist." He texts me when he is served a particularly heinous rendition, which generally happens in Minnesota. Here are the last three texts:

▾ Plastic cup of ice, half-vermouth, half-gin, lemon wedge
▾ (Bartender consults recipe card!) Plastic cup of ice, half-vermouth, half-gin, lemon wedge
▾ Real martini glass! Filled to brim with room temperature gin and vermouth. Olives.

The Midwest could use a little cocktail education. Still, the nice thing about sin is that it generally delivers. At the end of a hard Minnesotan day, even a cup of watery vermouth does the job.

There's a story in the Hindu Puranas about how the god Krishna's skillful drinking saved his life. When he was just a baby, an evil demoness named Putana was sent to kill him with poisoned breast milk. Putana assumed the form of a beautiful woman and charmed Krishna's mother into letting her suckle the infant god.

Krishna drank from Putana's breasts, but he sucked out only the sweet milk, leaving the venom behind. She perished of her own poison.

Discrimination is one of the qualities of the divine. Bartenders should drink the milk of the mixologists' techniques and fine attention to detail. They should leave behind the venom of judgment and privilege.

The granddaddy of the New York mixology scene is Milk and Honey, which has an unlisted number famously given only to friends, family, and the famous. Newer speak-easies create the illusion of exclusivity by means of (well-publicized) hidden entrances through phone booths or dark alleys. Anyone can get in, but the customers still feel some of the satisfaction of belonging to the kind of club that wouldn't accept them as a member. The "secret" door opens only for the right kind of people. I have no thirst for that. I came to New York to meet all kinds of people, not just the right ones.

In *Culinary Artistry*, the chef Michael Romano writes: "I think there's a danger of getting too much into the idea that 'I am an artist.' . . . A restaurant is about nurturing, about saying, 'Welcome to my home.' It's an interactive process in which you provide your guests with something they're going to ingest, going to put in their bodies. It's a very intimate thing, and they should have a say in it. Chefs should be flexible."

So should we all. Drinkers should try new things, even if they aren't "the usual." Bartenders should honor the spirit of the public house, a place with wide-open doors.

karen renner

▼ The Cocktail as Fashion Accessory

A (Very) Brief Personal History
Told through Drink

I have no style when it comes to either clothing or cocktails.

I will stand for hours in front of mirrors wondering how far the green shade of my skirt can deviate from the green of my shoes without signaling an utter lack of refinement. I flip frantically through makeup charts, trying to figure out if Hot Toffee eye shadow coordinates with Toasted Almond lipstick or just sounds like a delicious combination. I own two handbags (if you count my backpack), I never wear perfume, and ponytail holders are typically my sole adornments. I couldn't identify a Coach purse in a lineup, nor do I know if Coach actually commands respect, and I wouldn't have a clue if I came across a Good Find in T.J. Maxx. I know that brand names are declarations of personality, but I don't speak designer and can't find anyone willing to translate.

I feel the same anxiety when I order drinks. What does it mean if I prefer Shiraz to Pinot Noir, a Riesling to a Sauvignon Blanc? I'm absolutely fine with drinking warm beer, canned beer, and American beer, but because I know that none of these will do, I try ales and stouts and porters on for size. It feels like I'm wearing someone else's clothes.

What I have wanted all my life is not so much haute couture as the nonchalance of the well-dressed. For a similar reason, I spent a long time searching for a signature cocktail. It didn't matter so much what the actual drink was, only that it be unabashedly mine, so much so that bartenders would start mixing it the minute I walked through the door.

During my first decade of legal drinking, I tried on several cocktails to see if they'd fit. I knew subconsciously even then that cocktails are an important fashion accessory, a proclamation of identity and intent.

My mother had taught me well. Alcohol was her mood ring. Two beers translated into: *I was once a very attractive young woman.* Four: *I'm not kidding. I wore a size two.* Six: *This is not the life I was supposed to lead.* My mother had drawers full of Lancôme, purses in all colors, and a closet full of high heels. What a disappointment I must have been, with my softball cleats and baseball hats, my clumsy applications of eye shadow and blush, and my complete indifference to jewelry. My mother washed my hair with chamomile to bring out my highlights, slathered clay masks on my face to tighten my pores, clamped bracelets on my wrists and thrust gold hoops through my earlobes. She would save herself, it seemed, by successfully cosmeticizing and accessorizing me.

What I was seeking in trying to find my own rendition of "shaken, not stirred" was the poise of James Bond, the assuredness of someone who really knows who she is and doesn't apologize for it. Who is 007 anyway but a man who embodies the savoir-faire of the tuxedoed, even when he's wearing something else?

The white Russian was my first attempt to make a drink mine. Remarkable, really, that I ever thought that sipping a cocktail bearing an uncanny resemblance to chocolate milk would ever be a hallmark of maturity. But that was sort of the point. I was going to travel the world and have passionate affairs with older men named Sven and Yuri who would find my girlish charm irresistible and rejuvenating. Looking back now, throwing vodka in milk perfectly encapsulated my ambivalent feelings about being officially adult. I was still clinging to the knees of my girlhood.

Gin and tonic was my choice during graduate school. Not just any gin — Tanqueray. Being specific in this way showed that I had been with other gins, all sorts of gins, and now knew what I wanted. (This was a lie.) Most important was not to leave the lime perched delicately on the rim but to crush every bit of juice out of the slice before ever taking a sip. After all, I was no delicate flower. (Another lie.) I read Hemingway in coffee shops, positioning the book so that others could see the front cover. I got engaged to a nice young man who said he wanted to be a computer engineer.

Strawberry daiquiris became my specialty at the cocktail parties I hosted after I got married. I served them with brightly colored straws to other twenty-something couples, the whole time terrified that someone would realize that my new curtains came from Wal-Mart or that the linen napkins clashed with the tablecloth. I worried that I would choose the wrong button on the blender out of the seven seemingly interchangeable options, and that one of the wives would gasp, clutch her husband's arm, and whisper, "God, Scott, she's *pureeing* the ice." We all wanted to grow up but were afraid we didn't know how, so we brutally attacked anyone who made us think we were doing it wrong by doing it differently.

In between grad school and more grad school, I waited tables, often serving my former students. I worked customer service for Birds Eye in Rochester, New York. I got paid ten dollars an hour. I routinely handled calls from clients angered by the late arrival of their collard greens or kale. I worked in a cubicle. No one gave a shit that I had read Hemingway. I put magnetic poetry on my file cabinets, and this confused and upset some of my coworkers. I earned a reputation for being an impossible bitch after three Jack and ginger ales, and I cultivated it. I divorced the nice young man, got a new boyfriend, and moved away, but not in that order.

I left my twenties still lacking my own version of shaken, not stirred, and certainly the confidence that seems to go with it.

And things didn't seem to be getting better very fast.

I was in my thirties when I ordered my first martini, a drink I had always avoided because I never felt qualified to handle such a fancy glass. They were on special one night, and I was with friends I knew would forgive me any inelegance. I was delighted by the list of choices, which read like a dessert menu. I debated whether to order the Candy Apple (vodka, butterscotch schnapps, apple liqueur, and cranberry juice) or the Jolly Rancher (vanilla vodka and watermelon schnapps, with splashes of sour mix and lemon-lime soda) and decided on the latter.

"And you guys?" the bartender asked, turning to my companions. (In retrospect, I'm sure she was smirking.)

I can't quote their orders exactly, but the first sounded something like a dirty dirty Absolut, no olive. The other one, I think, was "an extra-dry Sapphire, straight up, with lots of olives."

A similar incident involved margaritas. I ordered a frozen Razzberita. My friend asked for a Sauza Hornitos and Cointreau, on the rocks, with lots of salt on the rim. When our drinks arrived, hers looked like a cocktail, and mine looked like a Slurpee served in an attractive glass.

My friends' cocktails showed that they were sophisticated women who knew what they wanted from a drink. Mine implied a juvenile addiction to sweets. On both occasions, I felt like I had shown up at a party without realizing what the dress code was, and while everyone else is sporting cute little black dresses, I am wearing overalls.

▼ ▼ ▼

I have been dishonest.

There's a great scene in the 1992 movie *Singles*. A man approaches a woman in a bar and says, "My friend and I have this long-running argument, and here it is. He says that when you come to a place like this, you can't just be yourself. You have to have an act. So I saw you standing there and I thought (a) I could just leave you alone; (b) I could come up with an act; or (c) I could just be myself. I chose c. What do you think?"

The woman replies, "I think that (a) you have an act and that (b) not having an act is your act."

Not having an act is also my act.

What, after all, am I trying to declare with my lack of fashion savvy except that I am too busy for trinkets and baubles? That I have no interest in labels because I'm entirely comfortable in whatever clothes I'm wearing? When someone compliments my skirt (the one that contains the impossible-to-match shade of green, for example), I say things like, "God, I think I've had this skirt since my senior year of college." Is this humility? An admission of fashion ineptitude? Or an assertion that I have so little interest in these superficial matters that I haven't changed my wardrobe since I was twenty-two?

In claiming for myself a complete lack of fashion sense, haven't I finally vindicated the tomboy who preferred catching softballs to purchasing bracelets and piercing her ears? I own more sports bras than underwired Victoria's Secret intimates, more pairs of sneakers than heels, and I consider my wardrobe diverse because it contains several differently colored hooded sweatshirts. At some point, isn't a purposeful rejection of style a style of its own?

For a while last year, I was in a writing group that met every Sunday at noon at the same bar. We even had a regular table. When I walked in, the bartender would pour a pint of Strongbow cider and add a splash of Framboise. It would be waiting for me at the end of the bar after I had set my things down. The Strongbow is my choice, a sensible drink for a girl who doesn't really like beer and has to remain sober enough to give useful feedback on essays that may contain words like "ontological" and then drive herself home afterward. The splash of Framboise was the bartender's suggestion.

But if I showed up at any other time, the bartender would have to ask what I wanted. I'm still likely to order a candy martini, only now I do so without shame. I am thirty-seven. I am single, and I have no children. Sometimes I drink a Jolly Rancher martini to show that I'm too much of a free spirit to settle down just yet. I refuse to act my age — life's too short. Sometimes I drink a Jolly Rancher martini to help me believe these things. Sometimes I drink a Jolly Rancher martini instead of buying a red convertible and dating a twenty-year-old named Amber. I also wear a toe ring.

I still order white Russians, but for different reasons now. They appeal to some sensible, no-nonsense, Type-A tendency I have to multitask: I will drink a delicious alcoholic beverage and prevent osteoporosis, all at the same time! And I like a gin and tonic now and then, but I have traded in Tanqueray for Bombay Sapphire, which makes a drink that, in the right light, is a subtle shade of blue. Alone at home, I'll fist a full quarter-lime's-worth into my glass and sip it while doing the dishes. I am still no delicate flower.

Nor have I shelved the Jack and Ginger. Some part of me likes ordering a drink that sounds like a mismatched couple from the 1950s who throw cocktail parties every month in their suburban home. I never drink more than three, though I sometimes like to threaten that I will, and I like it that those who know me know exactly what this means. I am Marion Ravenwood, throwing back shots against a man twice my size to win enough money to support my little bar in Nepal. I am the only woman who will win the heart of Indiana Jones.

The bartenders ask what I want, knowing full well that my choice will depend on my varying moods and needs.

Does James Bond have varying moods and needs, do you think? I mean, I know he has varying Bond girls, but aren't they pretty much interchangeable when you get right down to it?

Would you really want to date someone who knows he wants it shaken, not stirred, every single damn time?

Yeah, me neither.

liza donnelly

▼ My Mentor, the Cocktail

"*L*et's go to your house, Liza!" Those were words that I loved, yet dreaded. My high-school buddies loved coming to my house, and of course I liked being liked. Was it the Dr Pepper, chips, and cookies that my mother made sure were always in supply? The snacks aside, the big question was: how would my mother be? My fear was that my friends wanted to come to my house because my mother was kind of kooky.

In 1972, most moms stayed at home, at least the ones in my upper-middle-class world. So my mother fit in well. At least on the surface. What I didn't know was what was happening beneath the veneer of normalcy. It's not necessarily the job of teenagers to consciously know those things; their job is to be self-absorbed. I was pretty good at that, but I also shoved what I intuitively perceived deep under the covers. All I knew was that my mother was kind of odd, prone to say wacky things to my friends as she heaped warmth and care on them. My job was to be a good girl, the quiet, thoughtful child.

I can envision the wonderfulness of America right after World War II. We had won the war, there was money, and the men were coming home. Set up house, raise some kids, buy things — my mother followed the drill, and I imagine she did so with great enthusiasm. If you had a husband and some money, it was pretty clear how to behave as a woman. And in white, middle-class America, it was party time — what came next was a couple of decades of celebration.

The problem with celebrations is that individuality is not in the mix (unless of course you are the one being celebrated). The

53

1950s were a lost weekend that lasted for two decades. Toward the end of the party (I'm guessing 1967), if you had any notion of stepping outside and sobering up, figuring out what you really wanted, or who you really were, it was extremely difficult to do. It was even more difficult if you were a woman. Stepping outside the party meant stepping off a cliff, falling into an abyss. It was suicide. To heck with individuality; if you wanted to stay afloat as a woman, you conformed.

Around 1967, just as I was getting my first period, the country—and my mother—was disintegrating. Assassinations, stupid wars, corrupt presidents, "women's libbers" all made that too clear. The perfect life my mother and father had constructed created a satisfying career for him, a sheltered and loving childhood for me, but ultimately emptiness for her. My mother began to realize that she had forgotten (or had never been allowed) to find herself. I was becoming a person, and my mother never totally had. While the country fell apart, and I started my new life (as a woman), she gave herself to vodka. But I didn't know that. All I knew was that she was weird at certain times of the day.

My theory is the vodka allowed her to say things she wouldn't normally say, be the creative free spirit she left behind in the 1940s. Of course, it wasn't really her; it was the booze talking. Or was it? Like most women, I was determined not to become my mother. My young adult life became a lot of "nots." For me, that meant not getting married too soon, not squelching my thirst for a career, not inhibiting my creativity . . . not drinking too much. My mother died unhappy, and that was *not* going to happen to me. The embarrassment I felt about her when I was a teenager morphed into a burden of who I wasn't. Knowing now that her weirdness was driven by alcohol showed me that the big bad patriarchy—although not causing her drinking problem— facilitated it. The role that she was forced to adopt, that of homemaker, never allowed her to be herself. I would find a way to have it all.

Luckily, revolutionaries in the 1960s made that possible for me. The restraints on our generation were much fewer than on my mother's; I could indeed be the kind of woman I wanted to be, although it took a while for me to figure out what that was. Pesky feminine conventions still hover, and we are not unfamiliar with pressure to conform. But while the patriarchy shoved a lot of garbage down my mother's throat, I was determined not to let it pour alcohol down mine. The good girl that I slowly left behind surfaces every now and then, and when she does, I remind myself that she does not need a drink and can stay only if she doesn't interfere.

Who I am cannot be found with a cocktail. I'll drink to that.

▼ Hilarity and Mirth

Notes on a Lifetime's Drinking

Sometimes I marvel at how rich I would be, if only I hadn't listened to my psychoanalyst.

I went to one when I was a slip of a girl, the love of my life having refused to marry me unless I embarked on a three-times-a-week bout of Freudian therapy.

The first time I met my psychoanalyst, I apologized for wasting money by taking a taxi rather than the bus to our appointments. "Why shouldn't you take a taxi?" she asked. "You deserve it." I never got on a bus again.

Over four decades that's meant at least twenty thousand taxi rides—ten taxis a week, say, fifty-two weeks a year, at an average of £10 a ride—is that right? £200,000? You work it out.

Likewise, once when I lay on her couch, my sinews stiffened by a glass of whiskey before I faced a fresh bout of humiliating self-discovery, I said I hoped she couldn't smell whiskey on my breath. "Good Lord," she said, "why shouldn't you take a drink? You deserve it." I never refused a drink again.

The therapy went on for eight years, but her influence has lasted forever—if only in my expenditures.

I came to see whiskey as medicinal, for emergencies—but certainly I have consumed bottles of wine by the thousand since I left her, in the belief that I deserved it. Bottles of cheap raw red just make you liverish, and I soon developed a taste for the more expensive stuff. Cups of teas are just not enough. Wine is courage-enhancing. Good wine helps you confide your bouts of life-long self-discovery to lovers, suitors, employers, and friends, people who will listen for free if you entertain them well enough. You don't even have to pay them, like psychoanalysts.

Drink loosens the tongue: it has presaged every affair, every marriage I ever had. Way back in the mists of time, I lost my virginity to Cointreau, and just a whiff of the sickly orange stuff is still enough to make me swoon. Too much is bad, really bad, I know that, but just a little more than enough makes things *work*, speeds up the move from dining-room chair to sofa, from the back seat of the car to a motel.

Not a drop of alcohol touched my lips until I was sixteen and I was offered half a glass of sherry at Christmas by my step-grandmother, a wild soul. Even then my mother disapproved: she thought alcohol was a wicked waste, and she had seen what it could do — and indeed, since, so have I. Free at last and off to college, ignorant of alcohol's effects, I drank a bottle of cheap Chianti with a plate of spaghetti bolognese. I was sick as a dog for a week and have never been able to eat spaghetti since.

The only time I have been ridiculously, shamefully, and publicly drunk (that is, that I can remember) was in 1977, when I went on a cultural mission to Israel with a group of notable British writers; toured the hot, dry nation in a minibus with an armed escort; and after two weeks was welcomed back to the British Embassy in Tel Aviv for cocktails, where they poured us tumblers of gin and tonic in their attempts to restore us from heat and exhaustion. After that it was off to the Knesset to be debriefed by the minister for foreign affairs. As our delegation approached the building and ascended the broad, shallow, red-carpeted steps, I looked back and wondered why my comrades were on their hands and knees, then realized to my horror that I was crawling too. Fortunately, the minister was delayed, and aides fed us strong black coffee. When the time came for speeches, Iris Murdoch — of blessed fame and literary and philosophical memory — delivered the most impressive speech on the relationship between justice and power that I have ever heard. We acquitted ourselves well. Sobriety is a matter of will. I was proud of my country on that day.

I have celebrated good reviews and gotten over bad ones with alcohol. The stuff accompanies the writer's tour: it is evidence of hospitality and of approval. I have sat by swimming pools in the Bahamas and sipped gin and tonic, sucked up cocktails with little umbrellas at the Moscow Writer's Union, enjoyed the best martinis and the best conversation ever in Hollywood, toasted Russian poets in vodka, Finish writers in schnapps, and Australian publishers in Foster's.

I deserved it, didn't I? My mother said no, my psychoanalyst said yes: the latter won. Low self-image versus high self-image. Of course. Three words spoken twice — "you deserve it" — and if I had ignored them I would be thin, from so much walking and hopping on buses instead of hailing taxis. I would have married more prudently, I dare say, and been celibate more of the time and had fewer fly-by-night lovers. But would I have enjoyed myself so much? I doubt it. Would my life have been punctuated by so much hilarity and mirth? Of course not.

Nevertheless, at any social occasion that my mother and I went to together, she would put her hand over my glass and say to whoever was trying to pour me another glass of wine, "No, she's had quite enough, thank you," as she did with that original half-glass of sherry long ago. This went on until she was in her nineties and I was in my sixties, but I never minded. It's always nice to think that someone cares.

▼ Raising the Glass

*m*y earliest recollection of drinking was as I ate supper at my grandmother's kitchen table and watched my grandfather cut Italian bread by sawing through the loaf he held against his chest. Stopping just a millimeter shy of cutting his shirt, he would stab the tip of his knife into the new slice and drop it on a plate. Fine dining it wasn't, but it was great theater.

Having come from a country where even the cows couldn't be trusted, my mother's parents did not believe there was such a thing as "good" milk. They were also certain that if we ate milk and tomato sauce together, when they met in the stomach, they would "curdle" and cause no end of trouble. When their grandchildren reached the age of three, they started serving them meals with tiny juice glasses painted with oranges, filled with water and a tablespoon of wine. (Also, because our father came from a different village in Italy, they were sure we children were cursed with "weak blood" and thought it prudent to give us wine soon after we had been toilet trained.)

Perched on a telephone book, a dish towel tied around my neck, I would lift my glass of pale pink liquid and on cue shout "*Salute!*" Then I'd dig into a plate of homemade pasta and sauce, washing it down with water that became progressively darker as I got older. Life was ordered and sharply defined, with good and bad spelled out on separate sides of the ledger. Drinking wine with meals was just another example of how things should be done.

As I grew, my girlhood dreams were to be — in no particular order — a jockey; a water-skiing showgirl in Cypress Gardens,

Florida; Audrey Hepburn; and a bride. The pitiful reality was that I was a nice Italian Catholic girl on an extremely short leash who was continually warned against "occasions of sin," which I assumed meant events that took place after it got dark. My universe was school, church, and an occasional shopping expedition to Newark, New Jersey. Meanwhile everybody else in the world was having much more fun and eating meat on Fridays.

I was forbidden to go the movies unless it was to see the fake virgin Jennifer Jones look saintly in *The Song of Bernadette*. Patent leather shoes were too reflective, and wearing pants implied the presence of a crotch. The ultimate danger was riding in a car so crowded that you would be obliged to sit on a boy's lap. If a phone book wasn't available as a protective shield, it was best to ask to be strapped to the roof.

Since I was being groomed to be a wife and mother, just about anything interesting was forbidden—except liquor. When it came to booze, I could have pulled open the fridge in any house in the family and knocked back as much Gallo Brothers Chianti as I wanted, stopped only if there was a danger of not leaving enough for my grandfather. My father kept his liquor cabinet stocked and ready to serve his cronies without a thought of checking levels or counting bottles. There might as well have been a neon sign blinking "Open" above the door. The prevailing attitude about liquor was the same as for flour and Jell-O, with the assumption being that if you took it, you needed it for something.

It might seem inevitable that as soon as I realized there was the opportunity to drink at will, I would have run amok, but alas, there were no role models for such behavior. The women of my family were fabulous at demonstrating guilt, passive aggression, speculation, gossip, and scorekeeping, but not social drinking. For them alcohol was primarily wine, and they drank when eating a meal. Okay, maybe some anisette on holidays, but I swear that was it. They never—no, not ever—drank just for sport. The notion of a woman knocking back a martini was as disturbing as the idea of not being married before you were old enough to vote.

This made my high-school years somewhat socially backward. On Fridays when kids organized field trips to the bars in Staten Island, where the legal drinking age was eighteen, I failed to see the allure of driving to a grimy saloon run by the mob and populated by aged barflies just to drink flat beer. I could sit at home with my parents, watch *Gunsmoke*, and drink whatever I wanted, which was usually nothing because I'd had access to alcohol since kindergarten. Going to Staten Island sounded more expensive and even less fun than visiting Aunt Julia's.

As an adult, I recognized the joy of the social ritual of drinking with people to whom I was not related, but alcohol was still usually connected to food and company. Parties, barbeques, Christmas, weddings, and funerals meant beer, wine, champagne, and cognac. Drinking without food and friends just seemed somehow sad and lonely. Liquor was supposed to underscore the enjoyment of life, but it wasn't meant to be life itself.

My narrow understanding of the importance of alcohol was lousy preparation for the rest of the world. Without much in the way of comparison, I married a WASP boy child who I assumed shared my attitude about drinking. An advanced peek into his family's photo albums would have given me an important education. They were packed with pictures of bleary-eyed men and women clutching highball glasses and waving cigarettes. At the family's summer house in Cape May, they swung squat beer bottles toward the camera; on New Year's, they were shown in evening dress, toasting with glasses of champagne. I was thrilled at the idea of gaining membership in a glamorous, sophisticated club, devoid of men sitting around the kitchen table in their undershirts, playing pinochle, and eating salami sandwiches. It never occurred to me that my husband's family parties almost always included ghastly behavior and an argument about who was sober enough to drive home.

His mother and aunts drank with abandon, and it was at

my wedding that I saw my first drunken woman—who also happened to be my freshly minted mother-in-law. She draped herself on my grandfather's shoulder, gushing bourbon-fueled bonhomie over a man who hadn't bothered to learn witty repartee in English or any other language. Weeping, she called us on our honeymoon to apologize, a pattern that became all too familiar as the years unfolded.

My husband swore he wouldn't take the same path, and although he didn't suffer the same wretched, alcohol-soaked death as his father, it was not surprising that he struggled with alcoholism. Eventually, but not solely because of his drinking, we went our separate ways. I imagine he's probably living a happier life without me swearing under my breath every time I smelled scotch on his.

These days, with more of my life behind than before me, I still usually drink only when I dine. I love any gathering of friends and family where we can share good food and wines and tell great stories. The liquor we drink adds notes of grace and flavor to our rituals and relationships. I really don't feel that I've missed the thrill and abandon of drinking until I can't tell if I'm still wearing any clothes. It just means there are no photos of me splayed on a couch with my head under a cushion, looking like a dead dog.

This past Christmas night, we gathered at my son's house for a dinner of homemade ravioli. An excellent cook with a knowledge of fine wines, he is the father of two toddlers. We took our seats at the table and he poured the wine. Suddenly his three-year-old daughter looked at her tiny stemmed glass and said to me, "Nonna, I only have water in my glass." With a silent blessing for my long-departed grandparents, I reached over and added a tablespoon of wine to her glass, turning the water the palest pink. Then, along with the rest of her family, she raised her glass and on cue for the first time shouted, "*Salute!*"

▼ Where's the Party?

Confession: I like to drink solo.

My bad habit of drinking alone — and on the sly — dates back to kindergarten. Or maybe first grade. All I know is that sometime in the early 1960s, while my mother's back was turned, I furtively dipped my fat little fingers into the foam dregs of my father's beer mug to lick up the last of his Schlitz. The sour taste of the beer made me want to gag. But the thrill I got from secretly swilling a forbidden substance made my toes tingle. I knew I had gotten away with something sinful.

Which meant, of course, I would look for every chance I had to sin again.

Opportunities (definitely plural) soon presented themselves at the big, blow-out Italian weddings my family seemed to attend every weekend during the months of May, June, and July. At the receptions held at Frankie's Villa Pompeii or Amarante's-by-the-Sea, I waited until my parents got up to dance the Alley Cat. Then I snatched their souvenir champagne flutes inscribed in cursive writing:

Patty and Anthony
Our Love Will Last 4-ever

I hid beneath the tablecloth as I drained the last of their André Cold Duck, right down to the bottom of the glasses.

During my teenage years — while other kids filched Bud from their parents' basement refrigerator and then TP-ed the science teacher's house — I held myself far above such rowdy social behavior. I had a serious, Saturday-night job: baby sitting. Which meant I waited until those pesky kids were put to bed before I creaked open their parents' liquor cabinet and mixed half a glass of vodka (reputed to be colorless, tasteless, and odorless) with half a glass of cherry Hawaiian Punch. I downed the result in one gulp and followed it with an Act of Contrition.

My solitary drinking habits continued in college, where I attended a school that prided itself on "individualism" (in other words, the student body swilled the juice of psilocybin mushrooms in their dorm rooms instead of hanging out around the beer keg). Onward to my professional life as a teacher, where I never once joined my graduate students at the bar after our writing workshop (yet the minute I got home, I poured myself some Pinot Grigio and admired how it glittered like gold in the goblet). Even at academic conferences — known to be booze-laden events — I wait until the afternoon sessions are over and then crawl back to my hotel room. Only then do I bust open the minibar to treat myself to a mediocre twelve-dollar Chardonnay that I could have drunk downstairs for free at the complimentary wine-and-cheese reception.

There's only one place on the planet where I'll give myself permission to drink myself silly in public. It's a hot place. A dry (climate-wise) place. Two thousand miles from home. Three-quarters of a continent away from the censorious looks of my co-workers and friends and family. There it does not matter that (as the witty Robert Benchley once put it) "drinking makes such fools of people, and people are such fools to begin with, it's just compounding the felony." Here no fools actually know me, and even if they did, they too are fifty-two sheets to the wind.

Welcome to Vegas!

▼ ▼ ▼

Every year I run away from home with my sister and spend Labor Day weekend in Sin City. Gone is the laundry. Gone the dirty dishes. *Adios*, demanding husband and whiny kids and uptight co-workers who talk in MLA-formatted footnotes! *Hola*, alcohol! And plenty of it!

No sooner do Sis and I plop our luggage in our ninety-nine-dollar-a-night hotel room than we get to work on wetting our whistles. We head to the Venetian Hotel, where we sit on a faux Mexican patio watching faux gondolas float down the faux Grand Canal. We are drinking margaritas—on the rocks, not frozen, with a rim of copious salt—ostensibly to stave off dehydration in the desert heat.

But really we're just trying to get south of the border as fast as we can, without losing our chips and salsa in the overly chlorinated waters of the Venetian's Grand Canal. Here I prove myself a cheap date. It only takes one margarita to loosen my tongue to the point where I utter the first besotted thing that pops into my imagination.

Confessions: Yes, I have been known to ask the hot waiter, "Are you single?"

Yes, I have licked the rim of my margarita glass and said, "Wow, I've never tasted such salty . . . *salt*."

Yes, I have spat out an ice cube and then demonstrated Exhibit A to the astonished diners at the next table: "Hey look, this ice cube is shaped just like Condoleezza Rice's head!"

Yes, I have uttered the following moronic lines: "Whyzzit called triple sex? I mean, sec? Why'd I become a perfesser when I cudda been a go-go dancer? What's Acapulco doing in Mexico, anyway? Dontcha think it oughta be in, like, Hawaii? Whyzit called he-donism instead of she-done-ism?"

Should you care to join me in the city where everyone is lit up brighter than the Christmas tree at Rockefeller Center, I'll welcome your company. How will you find me in the throngs of fools doing the drunkard's walk down the strip? Easy! I'll be the one standing on the Bridge of Sighs, calling out over Saint Mark's Square, "Where's the party? WHERE'S THE PARTY?"

nicole hollander

▼ How Drink Saved My Sibling Relationship

We are not those sisters who are best friends. We are not those sisters. We are never photographed and interviewed for those coffee-table books about the special bond between sisters.

We are sisters who have fights in restaurants and carry on, shouting invective in the middle of busy streets in those rare times that we are together alone. We spend years not talking and ignoring e-mail messages and having terse phone conversations. She accuses me of leaving her wedding insultingly early. I am amazed I went at all. She married three times; surely I've done enough.

Sometimes we fight over who looks more like my mother. These fights are not serious. Both of us would rather resemble Lon Chaney.

My sister is staying at my house. I don't want to go into why she is staying at my house. But it's Christmas, and that has something to do with it. She has just come back from an evening with her oldest son and his new wife. She has had too much to drink. She has come back singing the praises of her new daughter-in-law's sensitivity and intelligence. Oh yeah, she is seven sheets to the wind.

I shout to her that I am working and will be with her in a bit. I tell her to watch television. This is cruel. She never watches television, hates it and doesn't even know how to turn the set on.

Suddenly she feels a drunken need for biscotti and cannot wait another moment. She races through the hallway to the kitchen, cleverly getting her bare toe caught under the cat gate—a feat no one could accomplish while sober. The gate flies up in the air in one direction and she in another. Terrific crash. She says calmly: "I have broken my finger." Indeed.

She insists I drive her car to Northwestern to the emergency room. Recently my car was stolen and then torched. The arson investigator tells me this happens four times a week in Chicago, but he has no idea why.

I learned to drive at age twenty-seven. Really that's too late. I'm not good at it. I hate driving. I drive through alleys and on side streets in my neighborhood. I don't venture into new areas. I don't drive on highways. The idea of driving someone else's car to a strange place reached by a highway is not something I would consider for a moment. She insists I drive her car to Northwestern Hospital. It seems to me she is not in a position to insist on anything.

I call a taxi and take her to a hospital that's near me. Everyone seems quite pleasant there, but the décor is not quite up to Northwestern's. It's a bit seedy. The adorable intern's hair needs to be washed. He instructs the lesser intern in pulling my sister's finger back into place. The novice intern is not a natural. She has to do it twice. It's not totally successful. I would have had her try one more time.

When my sibling tells the story of the accident now, she tells the truth. I am amazed. "Don't do that." I say, "It makes you look bad. Tell them you were rescuing a puppy from a vicious gang of puppy stealers who were going to train him to battle the rabid dogs of football players in illicit fight clubs or something, but don't say you fell on the way to get a cookie." I date our ancient friendship from that moment.

Now my sister's little finger leans away from the others. I feel a bit bad whenever she points it out. I never notice it on my own. Perhaps they would have done it better over at the more expensive hospital, the one near the lake.

We have become friends. We don't discuss our newfound friendship much. We just say: "It's a miracle."

She's sitting on my couch and she looks at her hands. "I hated my hands," she says. "They're just like mom's." She looks at her deformed finger and smiles. "Now they don't look anything like hers." She looks at her other hand and places it under her leg. "If I don't count this one."

▼ Sun over the Yardarm

i learned to drink wine from my mother-in-law, Sydney. At the time, I was thirty-two, had been married to her son for three years, and was a new mother.

From the moment Sydney and I became part of each other's lives, she has always gone out of her way to find something in common with me. She tagged along when I went to mass even though she is Jewish. She took Tagalog lessons at New York University even though we spoke English to one another. This was short-lived, however. Tagalog syllables and rolling r's interfered with her natural midwestern accent. Then she heard me yell at my child in Tagalog, effectively putting an end to any desire on her part to go on with her lessons.

To her credit, she found other things for us to do together.

On a visit with us one day, she declared without my asking: "I'll teach you how to knit. It's so easy!" She promptly pulled balls of yarn and needles from her bag, picking out colors that might go into my husband's scarf though he didn't ask for one. She sat next to me and helped me get started — "let's just start you on knitting, no need to purl until you're more advanced" — guiding me along as my fingers tripped and fumbled with two needles.

Sydney worked on her own knitting project while keeping an eye on my progress. The scarf ended up being close to four feet long and keeps my husband's neck very warm in the winter. I have not picked up the needles since.

She also tried to get me interested in sewing and bought me a sewing machine to get me started. I didn't get very far. I left it by accident on the sidewalk as I was unloading my car, and by the time I remembered the machine, it was long gone. To her credit, she good-naturedly replaced it the next day. More than twenty years later, the machine sits in the corner of my utility room and gets used only when Sydney comes to visit and I ask her to hem something for me.

Next came gardening, but I belong to the school of How to Hire a Gardener in a Snap and If a Plant Can't Survive, It Doesn't Deserve to Live. There came a point in my life when both Sydney and my husband banned me from touching any of our houseplants, which tended to wilt as soon as they saw me coming. I began to question my effect on people.

But in wine, we finally found something we could share, though I doubt my mother-in-law planned it that way. As with most things in life, it simply happened.

Between sleep deprivation, round-the-clock breast-feeding, the anxieties of first-time parenthood, the shock of seeing my postnatal body, and the beginnings of what would eventually become my first novel, I was a prime candidate for mental, physical, and emotional collapse. I was desperate for help but didn't know where to find it or even where to begin looking for it.

Sydney correctly and smartly assumed that a glass of Chardonnay would help. Whenever she'd come by for a visit, spend weekends with me, or have dinner at her home (conveniently, we jointly owned a summer home and we both lived in New York City, though in different boroughs), she would announce, "The sun must be over the yardarm." I learned that this was her cue to uncork the bottle and pour out the wine. In the summers, this usually happened around 3:00 in the afternoon.

What yardarm was she talking about? And what did she mean by "sun over the yardarm"?

I've spoken English all my life and pride myself on being a native speaker though I wasn't born in the United States. But this expression threw me for a loop. When I asked Sydney to explain the meaning of the phrase and how it came to be associated with drinking, she had no idea either. She did say that the yardarm was part of a sailboat.

On my own, I learned that the yardarm was the outermost tip of the yard (the horizontal piece of timber or steel itself) from which a square sail was set. In its original usage, the phrase referred to the time of day when it was acceptable to have an alcoholic beverage, usually around 11:00 a.m. But the actual time depended on the sun's ascent past a particular yard, the ship's latitude and heading, and the height of her masts. In contemporary usage, the phrase refers to the time that it is acceptable to have a drink.

Clearly, the lack of a proper definition did not deter us from drinking, though it was a slow start for me.

I grew up in Manila and was educated in private Catholic schools where the nuns taught us that drinking alcohol was the short route to hell, no visas required. Not that this stopped any of my friends from experimenting with and enjoying the different states of inebriation that alcohol had to offer. I could have kept up with them, but frankly, I didn't like the taste. Most of all, I didn't like what my friends turned into under the influence of alcohol — which was mostly loud and silly.

But then I moved to New York in my late twenties and found myself exposed to a whole different world of drinking, where an occasional sip didn't mean blowing up in smoke. I also learned that one didn't necessarily become loud and silly except by choice. As a rookie however, I usually nursed a single cocktail that someone else had ordered for me. I became adept at saying, "Give me one of those, too."

My first forays into drinking were not very successful, I'm afraid. I made the mistake of sipping champagne at a wedding, not knowing that alcohol and antihistamines do not go together. Despite my valiant efforts to run to the ladies room, I managed to throw up my entire dinner behind one of the food stations.

To Sydney's credit, she was a gentle and patient teacher. She never pushed, never rushed. She cajoled maybe, but she never threatened to pour the bottle's entire contents down my throat. While her commitment to my wine education was unwavering, she also had the good sense to go easy. I couldn't have asked for a better mentor.

The truth was, the nuns of my childhood continued to haunt me. To my uneducated taste buds, that fine Chardonnay might as well have been soda. But I didn't want to be rude and have Sydney drink alone because she clearly enjoyed her wine and the company. My husband preferred his wine red, and since his mother only drank white, he chose to abstain. He also probably recognized that someone had to remain sober around his mother and his wife.

So there we were, she and I, each with a drink though mine would sit in my glass longer than hers. She would always ask what I thought, and I usually replied that it was fine even if I only half meant it. Occasionally, I would break out into a rash. "Hmm, you might be allergic to sulfites," she would say and next time open a bottle that didn't have any.

I don't think she meant to teach me how to drink in any formal, structured way. She's not an oenophile. I don't think she needed a drinking companion either because she was doing just fine long before I came into the picture. But frankly, who wants to drink alone? Not only was I too happy to oblige, I was good and ready to learn.

Together, Sydney and I went through California Chardonnays, Italian Pinot Grigios and Soaves, French Sauvignon Blancs, and eventually the Sancerres, which I have to say is my favorite grape. That I can even admit to having a favorite grape is a testament of my fine education.

The more Sydney poured, the more I drank, sulfites be damned. Eventually, I learned how to drink on my own, buy my own wine, each time sharing my discoveries with her — "Chilean wines are great!" I was so proud the day I walked into a liquor store all by myself and bought my first case of wine.

Though I have branched out to different drinking partners, I have mostly stuck to white wine. Occasionally I will drink a red to keep my husband company. I have been known to say, "The sun is over the yardarm" — and I know exactly what it means.

▼ The Foreign Girl's Tour of Japanese Night Life

Welcome to Japan! This is not the tour you're going to plan to take when you first read this guidebook. You will plan on the tour of Japanese literary history or the tour of Japanese regional cuisine. These are the Japanese cultural elements that you talked about in your job interview. But you will take this tour, so plan ahead. Buy some cute tops and know that you start feeling the effects of alcohol after exactly three cocktails. Expect the journey between stops on the tour to take weeks or even months, and feel free to make stops on other tours in the meantime. If this is the only tour you take while you're in Japan, your priorities are screwed up, but your priorities are equally out of whack if you skip it.

Our tour begins in an all-night karaoke complex somewhere in Tokyo. The guide need not be more specific because you will ride the subway (*chikatetsu*) with locals, already a little drunk, and as a result be oblivious to the exact location of the complex. Fortunately, you were forced in Japanese class to memorize the relevant question—*Chikatetsu wa doko desu ka?*—and that can be answered by means of gestures and smiles. It should be noted, however, that the Japanese give terrible directions. If they say the subway is just past the Circle K, ask for further clarification, as you will pass three other Circle K's before reaching the one they mean. Perhaps of greater urgency is the fact that all of Japan shuts down at midnight, and even here, in the largest metropolitan area in the world, there are no trains after that until 5:00 a.m.

All of this is ultimately irrelevant, as you will have paid ¥4,000 (about $38) for the entire night, and you will be damned if you don't get your money's worth. The Japanese sense of privacy extends to karaoke rooms that can be rented by the hour—"karaoke boxes"—so only your friends can hear you murder ABBA's greatest hits. The price generally includes all the sweet, watery cocktails you can drink.

The woman whose floor you are crashing on will have gone home by now. You will regret failing to insist on going back with her, even though it was only 2:00 in the morning and you were still having fun. You will wonder if she will really be awake to let you in, and you will hope that she has not instead stationed at the door to greet you her creepy male Japanese housemate, the one who was putting moves on you before. That would be awkward.

Pass the time between whenever now is and dawn drinking green melon chu-his and singing Elton John duets with the gay Australian guy whom you have no chance of ever encountering again. Until dawn, he is your best friend, and you are invited to each other's weddings. You will make many one-night friends like him in Japan. Enjoy them in the knowledge that they are ephemeral.

Do not expend too much effort in avoiding Mara, the woman who has been flirting with you all weekend. By now, you will know that she is almost forty, although she looks younger than you. She has lived in Tokyo since you were in seventh grade. If women like her would move a little faster, you would have more X-rated weekends.

Mara will remember your host's address, so she will share your taxi. Feel free to chat with the taxi driver in Japanese about the town in rural Aomori Prefecture where you live when you are not carousing. It'll entertain the taxi driver and keep you awake. Don't hope to impress Mara with your language skills; she knows your kind, the precocious post-college girls who have come to Japan to wear out their wanderlust. She already will be committed to getting you home safely, and this will not be her last kindness toward you. In exchange for rejection, you will have gained a less ephemeral friend.

For your next stop, head to Goshogawara, a gray blight of failed urbanization in the center of Aomori Prefecture's picturesque Tsugaru River valley. If you live in one of the smaller, prettier farm towns nearby, this is where you will wind up when you're so bored you can't stand it anymore. "Gosshu," the entertainment mecca of northwestern Aomori, has it all: a movie theater, conveyor belt sushi, a karaoke complex that looks like a castle, a foreigner-friendly bar with a 1960s Harley Davidson parked in the middle. There is even a mall with a Benetton and a Baskin-Robbins.

But these will not be your destinations tonight. Instead, you will spend the entirety of your dinner at the Italian place (Italian as in spaghetti with fish roe sauce and *hijiki* seaweed) trying to talk your friends out of forcing you to go to the foreign host bar. It is a variation on the "hostess bars" ubiquitous in Japan, which in some cases are practically brothels and in other cases involve women in schoolgirl uniforms, but which are usually just dark little rooms where pretty, desperate girls wait on sloshed businessmen. The one your friends want to go to makes up for its weak stab at feminism with a wallop of xenophobia; at the foreign host bar, non-Japanese men, mostly Brazilian or Filipino, wait on and flirt with sloshed *female* customers. "It's so much fun!" your friends will insist.

Do not hesitate to repeatedly grumble, "Maybe if you're straight." Be advised, though, that this will not lead to a change in the tour route. Kindly refrain from expounding on the sociopolitical implications of the foreign host bar. If your lack of sexual interest in exploited Brazilians is lost on your companions, and *oh how it will be*, then your philosophical objections will utterly transcend their comprehension, and besides, it is not that kind of night.

Do not dare to hope that the two straight guys accompanying

you will get you out of this. They will both be in the US Air Force. Brian you will have met at the Hirosaki Cherry Blossom Festival this past spring and deemed an honorary male lesbian by the end of the evening. Chip, who runs the radio station at the Air Force base, will be new to you. You are advised to ask Brian to pretend to be your boyfriend in order to keep the "hosts" away from you, although you should not count on him to do a convincing job.

The "host" assigned to you will be Indonesian. Your Japanese will be more confident than his English, by a fair margin, but he will want to do this in English—perhaps as a point of pride, or perhaps because he has been instructed to. Order a Coke to settle your morally tumultuous stomach. Edge away from your host, toward Brian, who will be no help at all. Allow the host's attempts at small talk to degenerate into awkward silence. "I'm sorry," your host will say. "I see you don't like it, but I have to do this."

Recognize how high up in the foreigner hierarchy you are: a college-educated, Japanese-proficient North American with a renewable work visa and a government-sponsored teaching job.

"Do you want to go have a cigarette?" Chip will ask softly enough to evade the ears of the three girls who are enjoying themselves. Wait until you get outside to tell him you don't smoke. Instead of commenting straightforwardly on his heroic nature, let him lend you his scarf. Watch him smoke and ask him questions about the Air Force until Brian brings welcome tidings: he has told the girls to meet you at the motorcycle bar.

Chip will be sent to Iraq within a year. Hold onto his scarf. It will accompany you back to America, and you will unpack it in every new apartment. Don't wear it. Made of heavy, military-issue wool, it will be too warm for any occasion, and you will put yourself in danger of losing it.

Some months later, return to the bright lights of Tokyo for your third stop. This time, the destination is Shinjuku ni-chome, Tokyo's answer to Chelsea or Boystown, only with fewer Stonewall commemorative plaques or mayorally approved rainbow-flag pillars. The Pride Parade has not yet marched on Japan.

Descend into the only lesbian nightclub in Tokyo: Goldfinger, a dungeon of pop remixes and women who cannot dance. The exception will be a girl in a tie-dyed crop top and slightly cakey foundation. Japanese women are too shy to stare at your round foreign butt unless you shake it. In this nation of matchsticks, your hourglass is exotic.

Do not be surprised when the girl you are dancing with tries to pawn you off on her butch friends. This is not rejection. She is trying to figure out how to be polite about enjoying your attention. Gender roles are rigid here, even if you're gay — more so, maybe.

It will be too noisy to understand your second language, so your best bet is to flirt in Japanese, then await her response in English. You will get a kiss and her cellphone number. You will not forget that her name is Haruka.

Our tour concludes in Misawa, on the east coast of Aomori, where the Air Force base is. Make the three-hour drive through the mountain pass and the gridlock of the prefectural capital regularly because the girls in Gosshu wear you out (see Stop No. 2), and Brian doesn't mind smuggling you into the base supermarket, where you can stock up on whole-wheat bread and Mountain Dew. The little grocery store down the street from your house will have nearby farmers' surplus of apples and garlic, delicious locally caught fish with no English translation, and an entire aisle of Cup Noodles, but you will sometimes need to assuage your longing for crunchy peanut butter and sour-cream-and-onion something — anything.

After your trip to the supermarket, go out for dinner with Brian and Allen. Allen will have replaced Chip at the base radio station. He's taken a serious shine to you because he is the kind of guy whose house is decorated in detective fiction and contemporary travel literature, and there aren't many people like that in the Air Force. He might be the only other person in the prefecture capable of making a Chaucer joke.

Agree to go to the dive bar across the street from the base, the one owned by a forty-something biker-hippie Air Force retiree who never managed to leave Japan, and who now has a crush on you, undeterred or perhaps intensified by the fact that you have a girlfriend. (You do now! And about damn time.) It's the least annoying bar in town, and the infatuated barman gives you and your friends free drinks. Maybe that's the real reason Allen will let you spend two nights on his sofa.

But over *edamame* and variations on the theme of squid at an *izakaya* full of white families, the three of you get the urge to karaoke, and karaoke hard. Karaoke boxes are usually cozy (see Stop No. 1), but in Misawa, they are super-sized for the Air Force. By now, you will have a few songs that you know you can carry off despite your limited range and tenuous sense of pitch.

Brian will also stick to this strategy, but Allen will swiftly come unglued and start changing the lyrics to every song he picks. Specifically, he will turn every song into a rant about Heather (one of the girls from No. 2 — it is a small prefecture), whom he took out on a date with the intention of pity fucking, only to have her turn him down, a major insult since he is pretty cute in a dorky hipster way and she is bad-tempered, suffers from psoriasis, and looks kind of like a bloated Fraggle. Never break the heart of a sensitive boy because he will find a way to sing about you.

This tour will give you at least four great stories, but it will deprive you of one thing. When you return to America, people will keep asking you, "What was Japan like?" and you will not have an answer. They will want to hear that it was beautiful and that you had some kind of spiritual experience or cultural communion, but it will be hard to tell them that. A place can only be who you were when you were there, and you are not who they think they would be. It *will* be beautiful. There *will* be culture. But this is the tour where your memories will come from.

greta scheibel

▼ Sunday at the *Kilabu*[1]

*t*he rain played reveille on my tin roof as I awoke to another rainy-season Sunday in Ujindile. Tusker, my dog, tracked red mud through my shack until I shooed him back out the front door into the morning drizzle. I stood in the doorway and looked over the landscape that had gotten me out of bed every morning for the previous nine months: mist laying lightly over the peak of Mount Kipengere and its gentle green foothills — my own little piece of southern highlands heaven. Sundays in Tanzania are much like Sundays in the States: they involve church, alcohol, and sports. It's the one day a week when farmers, carpenters, shopkeepers, and government officials alike come together to pray, drink, and play their cares away. I, the lone Peace Corps volunteer in a village of 1,300 people, had my own Sunday routine: yoga, coffee, and an outdated *New York Times*; taking full advantage of the peace and quiet allowed to me by the preoccupations of my neighbors. The church bells rang as I began my yoga practice; I lifted my body into the Upward Dog pose. Positioned so Kipengere and the path to town were visible through the open door, I watched as women in brightly colored *khangas*, with children on their backs, gracefully navigated the slippery path winding downhill toward the church bells. The men, having no morning chores, had wandered slowly down the main road (the only road) earlier, hand in hand with their brothers, cousins, and friends. As I arched my back into Downward Dog, I reflected on the place of women in Tanzanian society — the con-

1. *Kilabu* (pronounced key-lub-oo) means "drinking club" in Swahili.

trast between their abundant strength and endurance and the little freedom they have.

I lunged into Warrior One, hands over head, eyes staring straight in front of me, out the window to my neighbor's hut, where the smoke from the cooking fire was dying down. A typical day for the women of my village starts with lighting a fire before sunrise. They wash and dress the children. They cook breakfast, clean the house, serve the food, clean up, and head to the farm. They till the land, plant the seeds, harvest the crops, and then return home to clean the children, relight the fire, cook dinner, and clean the house. They sleep a few hours next to their children and husband, then wake up before sunrise to start another fire.

This routine varies slightly on Sundays. On Sundays the women do their chores, go to church. After church, preparations begin for weekly village fundraisers. Friends and family get together to dance the afternoon away while the beneficiaries of the event accept donations for their children's school funds. When the sun goes down, the action heats up on the primary school's soccer field, where everyone gathers to watch the home team play visiting teams from nearby villages. Finally, the women sprawl out on khangas and watch the men play; in Tanzania, women are on the sideline. The men, however, spend most of the day meandering from the church to the bar to the soccer field and back to the bar. This point particularly irks me: after a long week working in the field, which sounds more relaxing to you — watching a bunch of teenagers kick a ball around, or kicking back a few drinks with your friends?

I pulled my arms down, into Warrior Two, and followed my gaze above my elongated arm out the door. I knew that down below there was peace in the village as the preachers preached, and the parishioners nodded in agreement.

I am not much of a preacher; I don't like to tell people what is right or wrong. As an outsider, one of my most effective tools in encouraging behavior change is my own behavior, leading by example. And so, as I balanced on my right foot and tilted into Warrior Three, I schemed—I would lead by example right down to the men's *kilabu*. I would put on my best secondhand '80s dress, kick up my flip-flops, and show the men and women of Ujindile that women are built strong, not to slave in the field all day and watch from the sidelines on the weekend, but to laugh, drink, and play just like the men. I focused on this as I stood up, tall and strong in my final Mountain pose. I was ready.

Within an hour I had bathed, dressed in a lengthy floral button-up dress, and was off for chai at Mama Jessica's house. My next-door neighbors are the best-educated members of the village; they're primary school teachers who have themselves completed high school. They like to think of themselves as progressive, and so I thought they'd make the best audience for my plan. I explained the details over a bowl of boiled potatoes. The plan went like this: go down to the club and drink. My plan was met with a string of "*ka ka ka*"s from Mama Jessica and Mama Chale. Mama Jessica nearly snorted chai through her nose as she leaned forward to slap my hand—her usual gesture when she's encouraging me to do something she would never do. Mama Chale grinned her beautiful toothy grin (she sports one of the few sets of full teeth in the village), as the men exchanged glances. David (Mama Jessica's husband) finished a potato and said, "Even me, myself, I will go to the *kilabu* today to unwind my mind." *Unwind my mind*, I thought; *my job does come with perks.*

After lunch, David and I made our way slowly down to the heart of the village. The rain had stopped, and a hint of sun strained through the canopy of giant bamboo plants—bending over us under the weight of the recent deluge. Bamboo, a member of the grass family, is the all-purpose crop of the southern highlands. It thrives in the wet environment and is used for everything from building courtyard walls and making musical instruments to feeding guinea pigs (which are raised for meat), and the most popular: making *ulanzi*, the region's *pombe*. *Pombe*, or local brew, is made by traditional methods from whatever crop is plentiful.

Across Tanzania you'll find *pombe* made from corn, baobab fruit, coffee, and bananas, among other ingredients. *Ulanzi*, bamboo *pombe*, is the unofficial drink of the southern highlands.

We arrived at the *pombe kilabu* around 4:00 p.m. Its location on the main road, within a hop, skip, and a jump from the churches, provides an easy commute for the churchgoing men. I could tell many of them had been there a long time. The line of men peeing off into the cornfield marked the entrance to the club.

The *kilabu* in no way resembles any Western idea of what a club should be. There's no disco music, no fruity cocktails, and no scantily clad youths. Instead, there's checkers. There's a large dirt courtyard, and a few kids playing with makeshift toys (cars made out of water bottles and the like). On that Sunday, there were two games of checkers going on, and many open doors. The courtyard, in the middle of a group of connected mud huts, offers a selection of different *ulanzi*. Each mud hut has its own brew, each with a slightly different taste. We asked where the best brew of the day was and were escorted to the dark doorway of a hut on the far side of the courtyard.

My entrance was grand—I ducked to avoid hitting my head on the roof while simultaneously tripping over a pair of skinny legs. I righted myself and said, "*kamwene*" in greeting to the wide eyes inside. A chorus of "*ka ka ka*"s rang out in happy unison as I found an opening on a bench nearby. The hut was dark, earthy, and damp. The small, lone window lit the 12' by 12' chamber, lined with low benches filled with mostly middle-aged men who drank out of one-liter pitchers. A few *bibis* (grandmas) who sat on the far wall, sharing a two-liter bucket, eyed me silently. The nearest *babu* (grandpa) took my hand in his (a common gesture) and exclaimed, "Grey-taa?!? You drink POMBE!?!?" His breath was heavy with *ulanzi*. Sitting tall with my legs neatly tucked beneath me, I replied, "It is possible" (a common expression). Everyone whooped and hollered.

The barmaid made a show of bringing me a small cup, the

size of a child's sippy cup. She strode toward me and bent her knees, bowing as women do when they greet someone, a sign of respect. I thanked her and raised the cup to my lips. One of the more intoxicated men, who insisted he was from Kenya though we all knew he had been born in the southern highlands just like everyone else, yelled "Careful!! You'll wind up on the floor!" and giggled to himself.

My only prior *pombe* experience was with *pombe ya mahindi*, corn brew—a taste similar to what I imagine fermented dirty-sock water might taste like. I'd considered this when I first pondered my plan, but I committed myself to drinking a full liter, just like the men did, no matter what the taste; this one was for the girls. The cup to my lips, I sipped cautiously. Then I sipped again, relaxing my senses. Pleasantly surprised, I took a third sip—it was delicious! I told them as much, "*Kitamu sana!! Nipe lita mbili*" (very sweet, give me two liters—in other words, make mine a double). David, my neighbor, leaned over and said quietly, "*Wewe* [oh, you]! You're going to have to walk home later, you know." I smiled. "Well, I certainly won't be drinking and driving," I joked, and I was rewarded with the hearty whoops and "*ka*"s from all who heard—there are no cars in Ujindile.

I happily received the two-liter bucket from the barmaid and paid her 300 Tanzanian shillings (twenty-five cents). At first nothing spectacular happened. The *ulanzi* seemed fairly weak—much weaker than the *pombe ya mahindi* my home-stay mother used to feed me at Sunday chai during my Peace Corps training. I sipped the murky liquid like wine, swishing it around my mouth and swallowing daintily; I couldn't help but perform for the large crowd that had formed to watch the *mzungu* (white person) drink *ulanzi*. My exaggerated sips were met with more "*ka*"s, hoots, and high fives from the *bibis*. Another few swishes and I had it: *pomegranate*, I decided, *tastes like a pomegranate martini*, yum.

Within an hour I'd drunk a quarter of the bucket. The entire male population of my village and several surrounding villages had made their way through the hut. I shared a sip here and a sip there with a few students from my adult English class and a few members of the dairy cattle group. Everyone was happy and spirited, even as an early evening rainstorm produced pools of inescapable muck.

The few women in the club were either *bibis* or barmaids. They sat silently and sipped their liters, occasionally dribbling on their once beautiful, now worn, *khangas*. These traditional, brightly colored and patterned cloths cover both their upper and lower bodies and can be used for anything from strapping a baby to your back to performing various house chores; I like to use mine to filter homemade lemon wine. Even as the cloths fade, they still add vibrancy and color to a life that can sometimes seem a bit dreary.

The men, on the other hand, were all wearing relatively modern clothes, secondhand garments from the past few decades of Western fashions that have found their way to the third world. A man in a "SpongeBob NoPants" T-shirt sat next to another man with a "Dick Knows Videos" shirt—both men looked to be in their fifties. A man I knew from the fishery group was wearing a lovely form-fitting, belted pea coat. A particularly tipsy man wore what appeared to be women's stone-washed skinny jeans, and the hood—just the hood—of a winter parka. The scene was the perfect reflection of the southern highlands rainy season—chilly yet warm, and always damp. No matter the season, fashion watching in Tanzania never gets old.

Everyone's attention had turned to teaching me to speak Kibena, the language of the local tribe (people in Ujindile also speak Swahili, the national language). On a good morning I'm able to remember one or two words of the throaty Kibena, only to forget them in the afternoon. On that rainy-season Sunday, well into the second half of my bucket, the words seemed to be slipping through my mind faster than I could slur through the vowels.

The barmaid brought me an ear of corn and repeated the

Kibena word several times. *This is a good word to know,* I thought, reflecting on how often I talk about corn in any given week — it's the "weather" of my Swahili conversations. A moment later I'd completely forgotten the word. I heard myself say, "Look, this corn's got hair like mine," with a big, silly grin on my face. The room filled with laughter. *That was stupid,* I rebuked myself. Another glance down at the corn, however, and I found myself thinking *but it really does sort of look like me . . .*

I had a quarter of a liter left. We were all sharing insights that may or may not have been jokes; we laughed at them regardless. I felt silly, slightly tipsy, very witty, and certainly not drunk; I had found my *kilabu* stride. Then Christian arrived.

As many attendees at the office Christmas party know, there's nothing that sobers you up faster than bumping into your straight-as-an-arrow boss as you're explaining the term "cougar" to a group of drunken men and solemn *bibis*.

Christian was silent as his eyes adjusted to the dim light. He greeted me in English (the star English student that he is), and asked, "Grey-taa, are you da-rin-king *ulanzi*??" I blushed, or maybe I was already a little flushed. In my most graceful special English (slow, drawn-out vowels for ESL learners), I replied, "No. I am just drink-ing wa-ter." He processed this for a moment, laughed, high-fived me, and took a swig of my bucket. "*Wewe!*" I scolded. "I thought you didn't drink alcohol!" Christian is one of the most devout Christians in Ujindile. He responded simply, "This isn't alcohol, it's *ulanzi*." I laughed, probably louder than I should have, and high-fived him. Together we finished the last few sips.

The bucket was empty. David had finished his liter long ago and was sharing with the *babu* next to me. I knew the men would carry on all night, and the straight faced *bibis*, well into their second two-liter buckets, looked as if they had the stamina to outlast even the hardiest man in the hut. Everyone stared at me, wondering what my next move was; I wondered too.

I'd done what I set out to do: walk the walk, talk the talk, drink the drink, and keep my wits about me. I'd had a slight advantage, that being that I was about a foot taller than anyone else in the village, and, unlike the locals, have a natural tolerance for alcohol. I hadn't made a fool of myself, yet, and this was in the forefront of my mind—even as I eyed the lone *bibi* dancing in the drizzle outside the hut and thought *that looks like fun*. I was curious to see what would happen if I had another liter or two, but that pesky fly of a conscience kept buzzing around my head: *quit while you're ahead*.

So I did. With as much grace as I could muster, I stood and thanked my hosts for a lovely evening. They thanked me in a continuous roar of drunken babble, throwing out "*anaweza*"s (she can, she can!) and "*nashangaa*"s (I'm amazed!) as I walked in a straightish line out of the *pombe kilabu*, into the dusk. I followed the cheers of fans to the school where the soccer game was still going on, despite the slick field and encroaching twilight. I greeted the mamas and *babus*, and a group of *watoto* (children). I tried my best not to breathe on anyone.

I heard Mama Jessica calling to me from behind. She was with a group of women sitting on *khangas*. Mama Jessica's smile was bright as day, though it was beginning to get late. I plopped down next to her, beginning to feel the dizzy effect of mixing *ulanzi* with darkness. As I told them about the *kilabu* they high-fived me and let out a stream of "*ka ka ka ka ka ka*"s that swirled around me. They could tell I was a bit tipsy, and spoke "special" Swahili to make sure I understood: "Next month we'll make your lemon wine and cook and drink all afternoon. No men, just us, a women's *kilabu*." I nodded as I pictured the women's *kilabu*: bright, vibrant, with toothy smiles and feet moving to music. We understood each other perfectly.

▼ Paralyzed by Fear No More

*a*fter I graduated from college, I was a White House intern in the Clinton administration. Yes, I was there when she was there, if you must ask, but no, I didn't know her. I returned to the White House as a staff member in 2000. White House staffers, even low-level ones like me, had a "work hard, play hard" attitude. Some of my best girlfriends came to town one Saturday night and decided to put this slogan into practice with me, so we proceeded to have a bar-hopping, intoxicating evening. As many women know, when you are drinking with your girlfriends, good conversation, encouragement, and humor flow even faster than the alcohol does.

I heard about how Leslie had gotten a much-deserved promotion at work. She admitted wanting to go back to school and finish her bachelor's degree. We were all so happy to hear it. Cheers! How Nadine was so excited by her new tattoo that she decided to raise her standards for men and stop settling for less. I was thrilled. Cheers! How Mikala and I felt like we wanted a life of balance and were on an endless quest for it, but we promised to hold each other accountable. Cheers!

The next morning, my eyelids slowly rose to greet the day. Instead of facing my alarm clock as I was accustomed to, I was looking at a hand. In fact, this hand came from behind my head and was resting underneath me. I went home with someone?! The realization was both an exclamation and a question for sure. I was not a person who had flings. I did not get "too drunk" and "go home" with people. Many of my friends did, but *I* did *not*. I looked at the hand: no dark hair on the knuckles, no ring, neat nails . . . Wait a minute! This is a woman's hand! Now my heart was racing faster. How did I, a "good girl," wind up in my basement apartment, on an inflatable mattress (not the fancy modern kind with a motor to do the inflating; in those days, I had the kind you blew up with your lungs or a vacuum cleaner, and I didn't own a vacuum—no good feminist then did), with a stranger—a *woman* stranger?

I began assessing the situation, which was difficult because the slightest move on this sad excuse for a bed, and everything moved. I was dying to roll over and look at her face. Did I know her? Was it one of my friends? No, I told myself. Mikala and Leslie were visible across the room. I could hear Nadine snoring. Wait! This meant they were there when "this" happened? I was regularly teased for being "too good." No more, now I would be teased for this very night. How weird that they were there for it. Was I good? Was she? Is she hot? Every time I moved a little, her arm moved slightly. I tried to listen to her breathing but heard only my own, along with my friend's snores from across the room. I wanted to put my glasses on to see the room more clearly, but I could only imagine where they had tumbled during whatever kind of craziness went on. The more I thought about it, the more excited I became. I still knew nothing about my bed partner, my lover, but I knew that I felt fine, even gleeful, and I must have enjoyed myself. And still I couldn't get comfortable with the idea until I saw who she was.

I couldn't take the suspense anymore. I was lying on my left side and decided on the count of three to face my lover. One, two, three! I quickly rolled over to my right and rolled right off the mattress onto the floor. I sat up. My numb arm lay in my lap. It was my arm. Not a stranger's, not a woman lover's, but *my* arm. It was asleep, so it wasn't moving at all as my body tried to communicate movement to it, and now it lay lifeless in my lap. I smiled, laughed out loud, and then felt a little sad. For a moment, I had been someone completely different. For a moment I hadn't been the "good girl" and had been free of everything that this good/

bad dichotomy implies. But like the unrealistic expectations I set up for myself, in the end I was left with just myself: the source of confidence and pleasure and humor and happiness and love in a variety of forms. I told myself to lighten up and allow for the possibility of a future stranger's arm, but chosen consciously so there would be no shock and wonder in the morning.

When I told them what had happened, Leslie, Nadine, and Mikala laughed as hard as they did when we were out sharing drinks, and they now think of me every time their arms fall asleep. Many people describe alcohol as having a numbing effect, but this was not one I was previously aware of. Cheers!

▼ On Saying, "Cheers!" and Meaning It

I had my very first drink in a bright blue, double-handled sippy cup. My mom's wine cooler was, to my fourteen-year-old self, irresistibly sophisticated: bright pink, and packaged in a big frosted bottle with a screw top. It was a new fixture in a new home, one we had just moved into after my mom and stepfather divorced.

I poured a quarter inch of the wine cooler into my little brother's cup, took a tentative sip, then spit it into the sink. Not because I fancied myself a sophisticate who knew better than swallow the libation she was sampling. And not because I disliked the taste, or because I was particularly concerned that my mother or sisters would be able to smell it on my breath. I feared consequences far more dire.

My taste test took place in the same kitchen in which my sister would regularly perform what Mom called the "pee jig," a sort of reverse can-can, in which the performer squirms and shifts from side to side while kicking her legs behind her, rather than taking a bothersome and time-consuming trip to the bathroom.

In short, we are not people who give in easily to even our most basic impulses.

Yet somehow my family manages to get itself into undignified situations anyway. My great aunt Jean went out for a fancy dinner, allowed the waiter to take her jacket, sat down at her table, and only then realized that she was wearing nothing but a dickie. The one picture I own of my great-grandmother shows her dressed immaculately in a fine outfit, with a stylish pair of glasses and a smart hat; her posture is impeccable, and she is sitting, of course, on an ostrich. My mother told me family stories like these to amuse me; instead they made me nervous. When she assured me that no alcohol was involved, I got even more worried.

Worse yet, divorces were not at all uncommon in my family (alcohol has yet to be entirely outruled as the cause of the unions and dissolutions), and I myself am the product of divorce several times over. I'd always imagined that "Product of Divorce" was embossed on the bottom of one of my feet, as on a cheap plastic toy. It indicated that children ought not gnaw on me or place me over their head; it warned that I had the potential to be very dangerous.

When I was little, my mother used to take us to our favorite bagel shop after she got her hair cut. As we were waiting in line one morning, I couldn't take my eyes off of the shop's business card, which had anthropomorphic bagels dancing across the top. There was just one card left, sitting in its plastic holder on the counter. I couldn't resist. As Mom paid for breakfast, I snatched the card and pocketed it. When we got into the car, Mom looked at me sternly and told me that I shouldn't have taken the card; there might be someone who really needed it.

I felt guilty for weeks, envisioning the poor, desperate person from whom I had stolen the card. She was doubtless unable to sleep at night, unable to eat, unable to carry on with her otherwise glorious life—what with the business-card-shaped hole in her heart, and nothing to fill it. I put the card in the bottom of the trash can and covered it up with tissues.

Heaven knows the damage I could do if slightly uninhibited. So I dedicated most of my waking hours to vigilantly policing myself. I lived in perpetual fear of being ridiculous, presumptuous, and overstepping my bounds. I spent a lot of time in silence.

A year after my taste of alcohol, I attended my first drinking party while visiting friends in Florida. Because I was far from home, everyone expected me to indulge. Instead, I nursed the same glass of hard lemonade for the entire evening. The last thing I was going to do a thousand miles from anyone with enough money to post my bail was imbibe something that would inevitably lead to my wearing nothing but a dickie and a feathered cap, riding an ostrich down I-95, littering the interstate with the forlorn bodies of all of my hastily wed ex-husbands, all of whom lost their business-card collections in our divorce proceedings.

It wasn't until I entered college that I began drinking, and it is no coincidence that a number of other changes in my life happened at the same time. My mom married a man who assembled an Ikea bookcase in my dorm room using nothing but a hole punch. Mom came and visited me over coffee. I made friends with people who always made me feel that, even when I lived alone, I was never coming home to a truly empty house. And I discovered I could disagree with someone in class, and this would not cause them to scream, cry, or burst into flames. If I stepped on someone's foot and only managed to apologize 34.3 times, they generally still recovered and went on to lead perfectly adequate, though maybe unevenly gaited, lives. As it turned out, I wasn't the Godzilla I had envisioned myself to be, leaving a trail of uncouth destruction in my wake.

Whatever common lore about women and drinking would have you believe, I didn't begin drinking because I was miserable and felt powerless and out of control, but because I felt the very opposite.

Nor did drinking unleash any destructive inner demons. In fact, I was a hopelessly cheerful drinker. I chatted in elevators, pushed cars that were stuck in the snow, and became an avid admirer of everyone's shoes. The only person I ever called up while drunk was my own boyfriend, and I did it only to wish him a good evening. Sure, I made a few typical mistakes, not the least of which was an incident involving a mesh trash can, but my drinks were never chased with regrets.

So let's enjoy another round, and make mine a double. No, no thank you, bartender; no coaster for me. You see, I have a stack of business cards right here.

kerri brown

▼ A Word for the Boys

How to Drink But Not Rape

*a*fter years of going undercover as a barmaid, countless late nights of fieldwork (followed by early morning hangovers), and too many salted peanuts to count, I have finally figured out what this country needs to end the thousands of sexual assaults that happen every day on our college campuses, in our towns, and in our homes. So I raise my glass and propose a toast—a toast to what change can bring. I propose that we (the responsible recreational drinkers) recognize that alcohol is a highly potent contributing factor to many sexual assaults today. I have also realized—after the occasional ass slap and catcall from my not-so-sober peers—that the problem often is not that women put themselves in tough situations, but that men make the situations tough.

Given that nearly all sexual assaults are committed by male perpetrators, perhaps we should refine our target audience. Perhaps instead of holding women responsible for protecting themselves (with strategies including walking in groups, carrying whistles, watching their alcohol consumption), we should redirect our attention to the real source of the problem. So here is a word for the boys—actually, the same words that have been used to dictate how women should behave. The following is a list of things men can do to protect themselves while at a bar or party where beer pong, kegs, and shot-skis run rampant.

If our society is going to treat every woman as a potential victim, then we must see each man as a potential perpetrator, right? Fair's fair. And since this method targets the roots of the pandemic rather than just putting a Band-Aid on the cancer of sexual assault, we may find it can achieve a success rate of 100 percent.

Instead of exhausting our resources in a time of economic crisis on self-defense classes, mace, and more of those blue emergency lights, we can direct our attention to the source.

Instead of warning women not to drink and get raped, let's counsel men not to drink and rape. Let's talk frankly about strategies and avoidance techniques to those who decide they are going to rape their friend, girlfriend, classmate, family member, or just some random person who happens to be walking near them.

Guys! Here's what you should do:

1 WALK IN WELL-LIT AREAS
Though you should try to avoid walking at night, we understand that sometimes this is impossible or unwise. Just make sure you walk in a well-lit area. This way, you are visible to others who are in close proximity to you, and they can therefore be wary of you. This will reduce your desire to attack, as you will be more aware of potential witnesses to your crime.

2 WALK IN A GROUP
There's power in numbers. So when you are planning on walking, especially at night, walk in a group. Your companions will be able to talk you down or physically constrain you if you feel the urge to whistle at, spank, touch, or attack a potential target.

3 WHEN POSSIBLE, DRIVE
Or if you can, take the bus home at night. Even better, call a cab. Maybe there is a friend who can pick you up and drive you home. Designated drivers are a must when leaving a party or bar. Not only will they get you to your destination safely, they will do so quickly and can offer a sober perspective. They may prevent you from hiding in bushes, luring people into dark areas, or stalking someone.

4 DRINK RESPONSIBLY

In 70 percent of reported sexual assaults, the attacker admitted to being under the influence of alcohol. If you are going to a party, limit your consumption. You are less likely to become violent, aggressive, and irrational.

5 ALWAYS KEEP TRACK OF YOUR OWN DRINK

You'll be able to track your consumption more accurately, thus maintaining better control of your actions. You will also be less likely to focus on another person's cup and less tempted to add more alcohol—let alone a little GHB—to someone else's drink if you worry only about your own.

6 KEEP AN EYE ON YOUR FRIENDS

You aren't the only potential perpetrator. Don't let a friend go home with someone he just met without knowing he has his cellphone, or without knowing where he is going and how much he had to drink. You wouldn't want him attacking someone, would you?

7 CARRY A RAPE WHISTLE

If you are at a party and find yourself in an upstairs bedroom alone with a woman who may have had too much to drink, and the urge to attack arises, blow your whistle. You will draw much-needed attention.

8 FOLLOW THE DRESS CODE

Nothing you wear will determine whether or not you're a rapist. The same goes for your targets, even though, when alcohol is consumed, a short skirt and tube top can be mistaken as welcome mats for groping. However, a good way to prevent an unsolicited encounter is to make your motives clear from the beginning. Wear a shirt that clearly states (in whatever language the majority of your peers will be speaking): "I WANT TO HAVE SEX TONIGHT" ("JE VEUX TE BAISSER CE SOIR" if you happen to be spending the night in Quebec, or "QUIERO HACER AMOR ESTE NOCHE" if you are in or near Mexico). This will clear up any confusion as to what your agenda might be.

9 BE FULLY CONSCIOUS

Be fully aware of the reality in which you live. Porn stars are fictitious. The dancers in music videos are getting paid to have alcohol poured down their chests. The dapper women in the Budweiser and SKYY Vodka ads are not only acting, they are heavily airbrushed as well. Alcohol is not a magical potion that turns any woman into a giggling sex-bot (so don't assume it will). While we're on the topic, drunk sex is rarely like the beer ads and music videos. I've never seen a woman voluntarily get alcohol sprayed on her. Alcohol is sticky and smelly—it doesn't quite have the same effect as Chanel No. 5. And after shotgunning a few beers, women seldom stick out their chests and suck in their stomachs (unless it is to look better than the other woman on the next bar stool, who is sticking out her chest and sucking in her stomach).

10 MAKE EYE CONTACT

A man is less likely to attack someone he respects as his equal. Try looking into the eyes of the woman to whom you are speaking. Try not to see her the way Frank Perdue sees chicken: as a collection of breasts, thighs, etc. See her as a person, which will be easier if you can master keeping your head upright and your eyes level. You can practice doing this while watching television, driving, talking with your other friends, listening in classes, and so forth.

Next time you're out with other boys at a bar, or wooing a woman with your finest bottle of wine, keep these "top ten" risk-reduction methods in the back of your mind. They are not meant as scare tactics, but rather as a reminder of the steps all men should take to ensure the safety of themselves and their peers. The steps shouldn't be too hard to follow.

After all, women have been abiding by similar rules for their entire lives, right? Cheers!

More Champagne, Darling?

I don't have any of those terrible/wonderful stories about my romantically tipsy parents, drinking sidecars, flirting dangerously and doing the Watusi while I watched, with nervous admiration, from the carpeted stairs. My mother thought that the greatest drink in the world would be a chocolate milkshake with a shot of Kahlua (and feel free to hold the Kahlua), and my father drank sugary white wine to be sociable (in later years, he just put a teaspoonful of sugar into the glass when people served something other than Blue Nun). They had a bottle of Tio Pepe in the sideboard for about twenty-five years.

I also don't have any fabulous stories from the time when I was a bartender. I didn't bartend in a cool, grotto-like place favored by hipsters and people drinking beer made in tiny batches by cool people in Red Hook. I also didn't bartend in places where I had to wear high heels, tight jeans, and a wet T-shirt while dancing on the bar for a bunch of yahoos. I tended bar for four years, wearing comfortable shoes and army fatigues. One bar was a dark, slightly mildewed establishment where three sad characters showed up at about 2:00 in the afternoon (an inept insurance salesman, a shame-faced classics professor, and the never sober, never employed black sheep of a prominent and industrious family). Everyone else came in after work for boilermakers or Jim Beam. Vic Damone and Frank Sinatra played on a constant loop, and to this day, I loathe them both. There were a few fights on Saturday night. The dishwasher had a .38 tucked under his apron, the owner's wife handled the cash register, and the owner's mistress waitressed. Most people drank in a business-like fashion and went home to face empty apartments or disappointed families. Some staggered out at 2:00 in the morning, and a few people vomited on me while I helped them into a cab. In the other place where I tended bar, there was a giant stuffed shark on the wall, the three sad characters were elderly lesbians, and the people who came in after work ordered boilermakers and sometimes rum and Coke. I got to listen to Chet Baker and Dusty Springfield every day, which was an improvement. There was nothing I ever saw or heard in either place that would make even one mildly fabulous and sparkly anecdote. It did reinforce my sense that drinking to get drunk was a bad and sad idea and rarely ended well.

What has saved me from teetotaling and my grim memories is champagne, "the only wine that leaves a woman beautiful after drinking it." (Thank you, Madame de Pompadour.) Champagne is my drink. I like the bubbles and the taste. I like the deceptively mild look of the chilled crystal flutes (not the seventeen-inch-tall ones and not the ones with colorful squiggles and not the ones with zig-zag stems). I like the excitement of popping the cork and the sexy struggle to pour the wine properly.

I was sixteen the first time I had champagne. I was working as a receptionist for a movie company, and a man who had produced what were called spaghetti Westerns asked me to lunch. We went to the Four Seasons. (I wouldn't even put this story in print if my daughters weren't grown women.) I had oysters Rockefeller and champagne and one of those charming little chocolate soufflés, with another half-glass of champagne. I alternated bites of dark fluffy warm chocolate with sips of champagne and thought, as people do after sex or heroin or sky diving, I am *alive*. I went back to work and noodled around, dreaming of my future life in Rome, until it was time to go home. The man came by for the next three days and we went to Nanni's and I had a Bellini, and we went to a little French place and I had a dish of champagne sabayon sauce over strawberries, and we went back to the Four Seasons for our farewell lunch and I had two whole glasses of champagne and another soufflé. He held my hand from time to time, and once he kissed me on the wrist. He suggested that I should not bother learning to type and should sneak into my boss's office and read movie scripts instead. He counseled me against hard liquor and early marriage. It was a very champagne week in my life.

When my best friend, a wonderful cook and a wonderful person, was dying, she lost not only her sense of taste but her ability to speak. I brought her handfuls of mint, cloves of garlic, a baggie of rose petals. On our last day together, I brought a bottle of champagne. She smiled at the pop of the cork and put out her hands to let me pour Veuve Clicquot over them, so she could feel the bubbles tingling. I held a glass under her nose and the bubbles rose up again. I put a teaspoonful in her mouth and she laughed, silently. One way or another, we finished the bottle.

In honor of the man whose face I can still see but whose name I've forgotten:

The Velvet Swing
6 oz. champagne
½ oz. port
½ oz. cognac
1 raspberry
Pour into a glass with a stem and drop in the raspberry.

In honor of my friend Amy Waldhorn, who named this:

Any Idiot's Chicken in Champagne Sauce
2 whole boned chicken breasts, cut in half to make 4 pieces
    and flattened with a mallet, then dredged in flour
4 tbsp. unsalted butter
½ cup diced celery
½ cup diced leeks (white part only)
¾ cup chopped mushrooms (mixed types is good)
¼–½ cup chicken broth
⅔ cup champagne
⅔ cup heavy cream

Heat 3 tbsp. butter and sauté all the vegetables for 1 minute. Add
broth and a little salt and cook for 5 minutes — no browning! Add
1 tbsp. butter. Add chicken breasts and sauté for half a minute on
each side. Pile vegetables on top, add champagne, stir in cream,
reduce heat and simmer for 5 minutes. Add white pepper to taste.
If the sauce is too thick, add more champagne, of course.

Serve on a bed of something colorful.

Everyone from George Bernard Shaw to Napoleon to me says
that champagne is the perfect drink. It matches your high spirits, it lifts your low ones. It offers comfort and a little irony in
one glass, and it calls up the deep and irrepressible bubbles you
have within you.

▼ The Good, the Bad, and the Bubbly

*t*he path to great champagne is littered with dead men, Françoise Duhamel reminds herself with a wicked smile as she fastens her seat belt and pulls it tight. She rarely flies, rarely leaves her vineyard, and already misses the wide stone terrace of her chateau where she stands every day, chin held high, dark eyes blazing over the estate her family has owned for more than a century. As the plane rolls ominously toward its inevitable take-off, Françoise distracts herself with thoughts of these accommodating men who died so suddenly, and so conveniently, allowing women to transform champagne into something cool, light and elegant, not to mention beautiful — it was Clicquot's widow, his *veuve*, who created the champagne everyone loves. Given the facts, Françoise thinks angrily, how did her stubborn grandfather dare to decree that a woman could never inherit the House of Duhamel?

Françoise declines the cheap, foul-tasting champagne being offered by the flight attendant. To drink that swill would dishonor her past.

To justify his insistence on the patriarchal line of the domain, Françoise's grandfather always proclaimed the authority of the monks who invented the first champagne — Dom Perignon being the most famous pedant among them. These monks were hardly angelic, just a horde of robed celibates competing with Jesus. Hard to outdo a man who turned water into wine, but they came close by turning black grapes into white bubbly.

White bubbly without the bubbles. The monks suppressed the glorious effervescence, foolishly considering it a flaw. Fashioning the drink in their wizened image, they not only drained the passion out of the juice, they left a huge lump of dead yeast sitting in the bottom of the bottle. A hundred years later, the *Veuve* Clicquot took care of that—she removed the unsightly fungus and let the beauty of the bubbles be. After Clicquot came *Veuve* Pommery, who politely attended her husband's funeral, wept for five minutes, and then marched into his *cave* to remove the sugar those sour old monks so sadly lacked. She gave birth to the Brut, which was far more memorable than any of her children, Françoise thinks with particular spite. Pommery paved the way for *Veuve* Bollinger, whose spouse died very young, giving her decades to refine the process until, well, Françoise. I am also a *veuve*, minus the dead husband, the thrice-divorced Françoise fumes. And I'll survive as champagne women have survived for more than 200 years.

Françoise was born and raised in the House of Duhamel. She managed the tastings by the time she was sixteen, and she was only twenty-six years old when her grandfather died. He bequeathed the house to his aging vineyard manager, but she contested his will and compensated for her "unnatural" place in the succession by working harder than ten men. She sold record amounts of wine, won more prizes than her grandfather had, and proved she deserved the land she'd fought to inherit.

And she'd like to keep on owning it, the fifty-year-old Françoise seethes, invoking the *veuves*, so much smarter than the monks— women who braved droughts, war, and disease, who survived and prospered, and whose pantheon she's desperate to join.

Which is why she's flying to America with her hat in hand, hoping a rich businessman from Houston can solve her woes. Nothing, Françoise admits, absolutely nothing could be more humiliating than seeking salvation from a box maker in Texas.

▼ ▼ ▼

One hour after landing, an impeccably dressed Françoise charges briskly toward the entrance of Harry Stone's surprisingly elegant home. She'd rather not endure a personal encounter, but if she has to meet yet another wife, she will. She's met so many, they blur together in her mind: the great cook, the beautiful children, the unbearable hobby—tapestry, quilting, baking; she's seen it all.

Françoise buttons her slim Chanel jacket and arranges the collar of her silk blouse. Elegance is her suit of armor, but her high heels soon sink into the gravel path, throwing her off balance. Before she has time to steady herself, the door flies open to reveal Mrs. Martha Stone, tall and wide, with freckles on her nose and large hazel eyes.

"Hi, Françoise," she says, emphasizing the *s* for so long it sounds like air coming out of a tire. "I'm Martha."

Françoise's slender fingers tentatively graze Martha's plump palm, but the warm Texan housewife insists on a real handshake, one that borders on an embrace. The cool Françoise recoils, awkwardly pushing an excellent bottle of Duhamel champagne into Martha's large hands.

"This is from my vineyard," Françoise says flatly.

"*Merci.*" Martha pronounces it like "mercy." "I love champagne to death."

"Then perhaps," Françoise taps the label of the bottle she has offered, "you have heard of ours?"

Martha looks at the label of one of the most famous champagnes in the world and frowns.

"Never heard of it 'til Harry told me you were coming. 'Course I got going with California stuff." Françoise freezes. Pearls before swine.

"Oh, I know," Martha continues, "you don't think there's any real champagne outside of France. But I did do the Dom Perignon and Veuve Clicquot, and Napa doesn't compare half-bad."

Veuve. Does she even know what that word means, Françoise wonders.

"Don't bore her, Martha." The short, barrel-chested Harry Stone finally appears. "Thanks for coming by, Mrs. Duhamel. In

Texas, we relax before doing business, just like you Fr . . . French, I heard."

"Call me Françoise, please." Françoise pronounces her name correctly, hoping Martha will notice.

"Oh Harry, thanks for stopping me from making a fool of myself again," Martha glares at her husband. "I'll stick to horses; you know anything about horses, Françoisssssse?"

"Let the lady in," Harry barks, his face reddening.

When Martha guides Françoise inside, her firm hand registers the sharp elbow of her angular guest, and she feels as though she could hide the thin, tightly bound Françoise in the folds of her abundant skirt. Soon after her third child was born, Martha's powerful appetite vanquished her minimal vanity, and she's irritated to see how quickly this stylish French gal can stir up that gnawing, long-buried insecurity.

As they head for the patio in the back, Françoise walks through an oppressive array of framed photos, a moist trail of Martha's maternal droppings. Children, grandchildren, weddings, graduations, sports trophies — every single minute of the Stones' offspring was not only documented but extravagantly glorified. Americans, Françoise thinks derisively, defensively — they have no shame.

Martha is about to ask Françoise if she has children, but before she can get beyond the "Do you . . ." something in the Frenchwoman's face tightens, and Martha doesn't finish her sentence. Françoise knows what she was about to say, and Martha knows she knows. This doesn't help the crackle of hostility in the air.

Françoise senses with dread that this whole trip is a mistake. There are no books to be seen, no art on the walls; the rooms are simple, cluttered, and lived in. A man who lives here, who has a wife like that, isn't going to give her a cent.

This broad is here because she wants something, Martha thinks, and she's as alone as they come, she's goddamned outnumbered just by me and Harry, never mind the rest of us. Listen, you skinny bitch, these photos you're smirking at aren't a shrine to fertility; it's a way of displaying the size of our troops, to let the other side know who's who, to surround the enemy if necessary.

When they reach the back of the house, Françoise is further dismayed to see a vibrant splash of color through the large glass doors. Please God, she begs, not another boring tour of a garden. But Martha goes outside alone, and just a bit too urgently, the screen door slamming loudly behind her.

"Mosquitoes are murder around here," Harry explains Martha's rushed and rude departure. He politely reopens the screen door and waves Françoise outside into the lush, bug-ridden backyard. The startling majesty of the garden shuts her up like a smack in the face for her arrogance—how could Martha cast such a spell on an ordinary patch of land in Houston? Feeling a presence as strong as the Duhamel estate, Françoise automatically straightens her skirt as if to line herself up with the sweeping rows of her own vineyard. Enchantment. Witchcraft. And Martha, now clumsily uncorking a bottle of California wine, such an unlikely sorceress.

"We thought you might like this wine," Martha says with a diabolical smile. "It has a story attached to it. We heard that French people like wine with a story, or is that just another stereotype they unload onto us gullible cattle ranchers?"

Françoise looks up sharply. She wants to respond in a clever way, but her breath is taken away by Martha's openly hostile sally. She's used to women disliking her, but not this fast. The moment takes place far above the short Harry's head—and his ignorance only heightens the clarity between the two women. Martha waits, and although her loose blouse and thick hair disguise her posture, Françoise knows her hostess's back is arched, and her ears are flattened.

"If your husband told you I am a snob," Françoise says slowly, "please remember that men are the worst judges of women. My grandfather would be the first to tell you that I know nothing at all about most wines. Nothing about any drink except champagne, and I was born to that."

Martha acknowledges the apology with a grateful smile. "I told Harry you'd probably rather have one of our native drinks — something you can't get better on every street corner in Paris. How about a mint julep?"

"I don't know what that is, but I would love to try it." Françoise can't believe the obedient schoolgirl tone of her voice.

"Much as I love champagne," Martha adds, "this drink packs a pretty good punch for a quarter the price."

"I don't think Françoise will like it," Harry says harshly.

"Françoise is brave enough to try," Françoise says to Harry recklessly, her disappointment in him as a cash cow rising in her throat. As Françoise follows Martha into the kitchen, she chides herself for losing control, for giving up too soon.

"My husband will have a hard time tonight with the two of us," Martha whispers. "Serves him right for dragging you here fresh off the plane. A cracker like him doesn't understand about jet lag."

"I'm not tired."

"People like us," Martha turns to Françoise with softened eyes, "don't get tired."

Like us. Françoise is amazed that Martha can say this out loud, and even more surprised that she agrees.

Raised in poor, rural Texas, Martha grew up around tough women: ranch hands' wives, subsistence farmers, women who ride horses, grow vegetables in clay soil, and live without plumbing. Raising her children in a wealthy suburb of Houston had been a combination of pleasant luxury and social torture. Martha had never had a manicure in her life, and she found herself shunned at parents' meetings and on the athletic fields, where she cheered too loudly for her children's teams. She spent a lot of time alone in her backyard, brooding, and ironically it was her crude way with roses that made the mothers come begging for her friendship.

Martha's passion for gardening came from a hatred of nature that few could equal. She wanted to avenge herself on the arid, dusty, flat landscape where she'd been raised and plant the flowers that nature had denied her in childhood. She counted the hours of sun and shade in her garden, made charts, and drew diagrams. Harry had thought this must be a symptom of early menopause and hoped it would pass. It didn't.

Martha ended up with a rose garden that became, as the garden magazines reported, "the envy of all the housewives in Houston." To Martha's greatest amusement, some mothers began to imitate her ranch-hand "style." Long, flowing dresses and sturdy sandals were now permitted at outdoor cocktail parties, all thanks to Martha.

Françoise notices the rebellious jungle of a rose garden when Martha takes her back outside to cut the mint.

"I've always hated roses," Françoise says sharply, "even ours. But these are beautiful. I don't know why."

"Because I let mine run wild. I cut and chop, but mostly I let them have their way," Martha answers as she points to one particularly wayward climbing rose.

"The opposite of what you do with grapes."

"Or children," Martha adds.

"Is it?" Françoise asks, and Martha silently accepts this admission of her visitor's childless state.

Françoise would like to lean her head on Martha's shoulder and tell her everything—how she'd been so busy conquering nature that she'd been undone by a simple man. The disinherited manager to whom she'd been so generous had cooked the books and robbed her blind. She imagined her grandfather laughing at her: *You see, even though you did a good job, the house of a woman will always fall. Even a bad man is better than a good woman.*

Françoise naively assumed everyone would help her save the finest house in France, and she was stunned when the French banks turned their backs on her. She started chasing money as passionately as her grandfather had prayed for rain. Harry came recommended as a sucker who'd give a private loan to anyone who traded in social status. But does the wily, unpretentious Martha disapprove?

Martha hands Françoise her clippers: "Do your own; it's more fun." Françoise hesitates. She's never dared to fool with any of the plants on her estate — she admires and controls but does not touch so much as a blade of grass. What if she cuts in a bad place and makes an unsightly dent?

"Mint grows like a weed — in fact, it *is* a weed." Martha sees Françoise wavering. "You can cut anywhere, and you won't see the wound tomorrow."

"Your husband is kind of like that," Françoise smiles.

"Yes," Martha laughs with delight, "you got that right!"

"You too, in a different way, no?" Françoise adds.

"Oh yes. You lucked into meeting the toughest bitch in Texas," Martha says, cursing in front of a stranger for the first time in thirty years. "I'm the only woman within a hundred miles of here that isn't intimidated by a beautiful Fr . . . Frenchwoman."

"Oh, go ahead and call me a Frog," Françoise cuts in. "Maybe you'll stop doing it behind my back."

"Damn!" Martha exclaims. "Aren't you a sight for sore eyes!"

Françoise cuts the mint brazenly, and Martha guides her silently through the rest of the garden. Turning right, the path climbs upward, and Françoise ducks to avoid the tall, tropical plants with bizarrely shaped leaves that appear as suddenly as a monster in a horror movie. The next turn brings swirling grasses and spires of blue that brush against her cheeks. Hearing Martha's reassuring steps crunch ahead of her, Françoise remembers being carried by her grandfather through the vineyards when she was a small girl, her hands clinging to his neck. When a vine came close, she hid her face in his chest, loving the smell of dirt on his skin, which she'd always associated with feeling safe.

Safe; what a joke. She'd never been safe.

Just when Françoise is certain that they'll never get back to the house, the stone patio comes into view with Harry sitting, glumly confused, at the dinner table.

"What the hell took you so long?" Harry barks at Martha as the two women appear.

Martha waves her handful of mint at him dismissively before going into the kitchen. Françoise sits down, facing Harry. Perhaps Martha lures all his suitors down the perfumed path, infusing it with her own warmth and promise of friendship and then, a co-conspirator, drops her prey in front of Harry, to do with as he pleases.

Harry doesn't know what to say to Françoise, whose desperation is so clearly burning behind her beautifully sculpted features. She thinks she can trick him, Harry smiles to himself, but he can smell the need for money from miles away. Especially when it's camouflaged as a "worthwhile" investment. If not for Martha's obsession, he wouldn't even have answered the call.

The sixty-three-year-old Harry has only recently discovered that people not only laugh at him for making cardboard boxes, they actually presume that *he's* ashamed of the way in which he makes money. Even more stupidly, they claim he was trying to class up his reputation by building that big new art museum, when it should be obvious to any good businessman that he'd done it for the tax deduction. Since then, he's been besieged by requests for cultural contributions, as well as loans for "upscale" (meaning risky) concerns.

Martha bursts through the door with two large frosty glasses stuffed with mint and bourbon and sugar, and hands one to Françoise. "You just might give up champagne for this!"

Harry winces as he sees his wife through the eyes of the sleek Madame Duhamel. This fills him with a sudden and unbearable hatred for Françoise that propels him forcibly into the house.

Martha shrugs at his abrupt departure as Françoise takes a long soothing sip of the sweet mixture. The unfamiliar taste of whiskey stretches from her front teeth to her toes. Unlike the languorous and polite intoxication of champagne, which builds slowly to a crescendo, whiskey takes hold of you immediately, separating the men from the boys and, to Martha and Françoise's delight, making fast friends of rugged women.

"I have never bought oil or vinegar mixed with herbs," Françoise says between gulps, "but this works, this mint."

"Because it's fresh," Martha says crunching a piece of ice loudly between her teeth. "You can't let herbs get drenched and then have them sit around."

"You have a lot of rules," Françoise says with approval. "This makes you an honorary Frog."

"Frog?" a somewhat recovered Harry says as he flings open the screen door and sits back down. "You call yourselves Frogs?"

The two women laugh, and a frustrated Harry turns in his seat to look at the widescreen television he had surreptitiously turned on, with the sound muted, when he went inside. He checks the score of a football game.

To Françoise and Martha's relief, Harry keeps watching the game throughout the dinner of grilled steak, baked potato, and salad. Warmed by the whiskey, they decide to have an after-dinner competition between French and California champagne.

"I feel sorry for you already," Françoise quips. "Sparkling wine is not champagne."

"Hold your horses," Martha answers, "before you regret your boasting. Plenty of your snooty competitors use our grapes, don't they?"

Françoise winces as she remembers her attempt at a partnership between her house and a California winery. She'd seen the success of her rivals but mainly hoped a new business model would finally secure a hefty loan. It didn't.

Never sleep with your banker's husband—Françoise learned that lesson too late. Who could have known how closely all the banks would stand by that bitter wife? Humiliation overwhelms her, and she devours her steak in anger.

"Don't tell me a skinny gal like you always eats this much," Martha says.

"I eat one meal a day," Françoise answers with a shake of her head. "The rest is coffee."

"Hell on earth." Martha swallows a mouthful of potato.

"Starving is easy."

"Not for me."

"Other things are easy for you."

"Like what?"

"Staying married." Françoise smiles.

Martha's face reveals that her marriage is anything but easy. "Let's uncork the champagne on that," she says.

"I want to see the last quarter on the big screen downstairs." Harry can't wait to escape. "I'll be right back."

Martha pops the cork of the California champagne and pours two glasses. She hands Françoise the Duhamel.

"You open this one," she says, wiping the extra foam off her bottle and sucking it off her finger. "Mmmm, you got some stiff competition, lady."

Françoise laughs uncharacteristically loud, her nerves fraying over Harry's clear indifference to her mission. But as the perfect French cork pops easily out of the bottle, her competitive spirit takes over. She at least has to win the bet with Martha.

A sip of the Duhamel, and she's a girl again, riding on her grandfather's back, the bark scraping her legs, breathing in the smell of summer, of lavender, oleander, and wisteria, of dirt. Another sip, and she holds her grandfather's hand as they walk along the dusty paths between the vines, eating a juicy peach, the sun burning on her face.

Martha almost purrs when she tastes Françoise's champagne —she's clearly falling in love. She savors it slowly, and then takes a long cool drink of her contender. Françoise feels certain of victory, but Martha refuses to surrender right away. "You ever seen fields of mustard?"

Françoise shakes her head.

"The yellow's unbelievable." Martha takes another sip from her California glass. "Especially in the burning sun. The light in Napa has edges, you know what I mean?"

Françoise takes Martha's empty glass and fills it with the Duhamel. She wants to tear Martha away from California and bring her back to France. She hopes the taste will make this Texan woman see and smell a place she's never seen.

When Françoise sees Martha smiling across the table, she envies her happiness as she's never envied anyone before.

The French is older and better, but in the end, they're more alike than different. The blended grapes, the lighter touch, the beautiful bubbles, two centuries of *veuve* wisdom had all come to California preapproved.

"So?" Martha demands her opinion.

"Your sparkling wine . . ."

"My champagne?" Martha jokes.

"Your Napa bubbly is good."

"Very good?"

"Very good."

"Yeah, but yours is excellent."

"The difference?" Françoise quizzes her like a schoolteacher.

"Mine is lighter," Martha takes a sip of each. "Too light."

"*Exactement!*" says Françoise, her language pouring out of her by mistake. She mustn't sound like a snob. Not now.

"Could it be improved — I mean, with what it's got?"

Françoise takes another sip of the California wine, then pauses dramatically.

"Absolutely," she decides. "The grapes are good, better than I thought those cowboys could grow."

"How would you make it better?" Martha asks roughly, demanding the truth. Is she angry about losing?

"Even with the pure Chardonnay grape, you have to do a second fermentation in the bottle. That's how you get the bubbles right," Françoise enthuses about the single passion of her life — a passion that always cut deeper than her feelings for anything or anyone. "You need great patience — no one in America is that patient." Françoise risks a jibe hoping to restore their camaraderie. "We still rotate the bottles by hand."

"You do? So many?"

"We must. Or my grandfather would rise from his grave to kill me."

"Tell me about this grandfather of yours."

"He was a selfish old tyrant," Françoise spits out, the first time she's spoken ill of him to another person.

"And you're exactly like him," Martha returns cheerfully.

Françoise is relieved to hear her friendly tone.

"Look," Martha taps the bottle on the table, "I own more than half the California vineyard that makes this stuff. It's the best the whole state has to offer, but with your help, I don't have to be satisfied with that anymore."

"You own it?"

"You didn't think Harry could care less about champagne?"

"He seemed to be . . ."

"That was because of me. He'd never invest in something he can't understand."

Martha had come full circle to honor her twisted roots in the dry and dusty soil where women never planted anything they couldn't eat. But Martha did them one better by harvesting what she could drink.

"I did not know I was discussing family secrets with a competitor," Françoise says coldly.

"Competitor?" Martha laughs out loud. "The hell I am. I've tasted most of the deluxe French champagnes, but yours beats 'em all. If you think my grapes are good enough for your hand-turning techniques, we've got some money to make."

The lighthearted banter is over. Guided by all the *veuves* who'd survived the violence of both man and nature, and who'd each found their unique road to salvation, Madame Duhamel had come to the right place for the wrong reason.

"I'm not into this just for the money, I promise you that," Martha tells Françoise. "I just don't want to die before I learn how to make champagne the right way."

"It will take time, remember our slow French time? But the money will be needed very fast, to *do it right*, as you say."

"All you got to do is share the wealth of your knowledge, leave the crude cash to me." Martha pats Françoise's hand as if she were child begging for more dessert. The motherless Françoise now revels in her touch — suddenly understanding, for the first time, what it might have felt like if she had been a beloved daughter.

Martha takes another sip of the Duhamel. "You and I can have a lot of fun, don't you think?"

Françoise nods, and above Martha's head she sees the *Veuves* Clicquot, Pommery, and Bollinger floating in the air. Clicquot has one of Martha's roses in her mouth and dances whimsically, tossing her head back with abandon. Françoise toasts the *veuves*, and then she and Martha click glasses.

Françoise imagines her leathery, silver-haired grandfather coming upon Martha in his vineyard. She's wearing her long dress and floppy hat, her hips bulging and her feet bare. Françoise expects him to sneer, *Get this amateur out of my sight*, but he doesn't. He stops, he looks, but before he can say a word, Martha slips by him, sniffs one of his grapes, and presses the tough bark of the vine, occasionally taking a handful of earth in her hand and squeezing.

Veuves. Widows. Martha has a husband and Françoise had three, but that matters little now as the two women empty their glasses in triumph, sealing the deal in silence, securing the fate of the House of Duhamel, every bubble worth a thousand words.

▼ The Breakup

*i*hadn't seen Eliza in fifteen years when, on a brisk and sunny autumn morning, I bumped into her at the farmers' market in Union Square.

"Eliza!" I said, turning to the voice that had called my name. We hugged and exchanged pleasantries before deciding to walk together up Broadway. Suddenly, she asked if I'd been one of the women who'd been in the reading group — the final one, many years ago now, the one that got the big headline and picture in the *New York Post*'s celebrity section, Page Six. I explained to her that she was right to remember I'd belonged to the group, but I'd stopped going long before that night when the group broke up. Did I know what had happened, she asked. I told her I knew there'd been a tiff of some sort that had put an end to the group. Well, Eliza said she'd learned all about it from the other Laurie in the group, who had been there, so she would tell me.

It just so happened that Eliza had recounted the story to someone else a few days earlier, and I could tell she was eager to tell it yet again. Frankly, I was eager to hear it. In relaying it to you, I'll probably mix things up a little, but I think I have the gist right. Here's Eliza's account of what Laurie said.

▼ ▼ ▼

Since you asked, I'm going to tell you all about what happened. There were lots of reading groups in the city back in the late '80s and early '90s. Our group was all women, and we conducted our discussions very seriously, almost as if they were college classes. It's true that we probably drank too much wine when we talked about the books, but we rarely got totally drunk. We simply believed wine made discussions flow. Whatever good ideas we had over the years came about because of the wine. But right before we broke up, the wine, instead of making us better at talking about the books, seemed to be making us do nothing but argue.

Our group met once a month at a downtown restaurant. As soon as the first person arrived, a waiter would bring two bottles of wine—one white, one red—along with a platter of hummus with carrots, celery, and pita bread. Most discussions lasted about three hours. My head used to spin like crazy afterward—not from the wine, I swear—but from all the hard thinking.

Phoebe, at twenty-six, was the youngest in the group. Petite and pretty, with bright skin and a lovely, shy smile, she wore the same kind of black-rimmed glasses Daniel Libeskind wears. She always seemed animated, even though she hardly gestured at all, and for some odd reason, she never showed even the slightest effects from the wine. Phoebe wrote theater and movie reviews for a West Side community paper, and her first novel came out right near the time we broke up. It was "well received," as they say. I never actually read it—such a jejune title: *My Lovely Jane*.

Olive, at sixty, was the oldest. Time had been kind to her, etching only a few fine lines around her eyes. A tall woman, she was what you would call "handsome."

At our meetings, the group followed rules. For example, we never chose books from bestseller lists. To choose a book for discussion, each person gave a two-minute pitch on behalf of a particular book. Then we'd ask questions about the book—comments weren't allowed. After the pitches, we'd write down our choice on a piece of paper. Whichever title got the most votes won—simple as that.

Our first book had been Edward Gibbon's *Decline and Fall of the Roman Empire*. All anyone could say during the discussion was, "Holy cow, things got even worse after that!" It took us a while to learn that we needed books we could talk back to.

The next book was Barbara Tuchman's *A Distant Mirror*. Although we learned the fourteenth century was full of beheadings, spearings, burnings at the stake, rape, pillage, brigandage—and, worst of all, the Black Death—the book loosened us up. After that, we found book after book that we could never talk enough about.

Phoebe and Sarah arrived late that last night, but it didn't matter. We were in a celebratory mood because Annie's new novel had just gotten a rave review in the *Times*.

Annie, of course, was the brilliant one in the group. She was a well-known novelist even when the group first started meeting. We were all in awe of her and wondered why she put up with us. She was our unspoken leader—the prime mover who got the group talking each time we met. Everyone knew that the group would fall apart if she ever decided she'd had enough. Though not beautiful at all, there was something about her that always made men turn to look at her.

Annie's fame as a novelist made her popular with the gossip columnists. *Paparazzi* were always hanging around outside the restaurant to snap pictures of her as she emerged from our meeting, usually wobbling from having drunk too much wine. Her picture was at the top of Page Six in the *Post* so often that we joked she was their logo.

Aside from Annie, Phoebe, and Olive—and me, of course—there were four others—Nancy, Barbara, Cinder, and Sarah. Nancy was a bit of a prig, always wearing Talbots jackets over matronly silk blouses. A successful doctor and married mother of two, she'd been Annie's roommate in college.

Then there was Barbara, who lived in Nancy's building and had a job as a social worker. She was intelligent, annoyingly intense, and rather plain. She had been married for twenty years to a weird guy whom she adored. Childless, the two of them smothered their five cats with love.

There was also Cinder—odd name, I admit. She taught in the comp lit department at Hofstra, a college just outside the city. She and Annie were extremely close and had grown up together.

Last was Sarah. Now *she* was a real stunner. With blue-black hair and poreless skin, she had one of those long Roman noses that made her look aristocratic and unapproachable.

That last night started out as usual. We spent a few minutes celebrating Annie's good news, with everyone repeating the same toast about how great a writer she was, and we decided to start the pitches even though Sarah and Phoebe hadn't showed up yet. It was Barbara's turn to go first. We filled our glasses and settled back in our chairs to listen.

Barbara

"I'm proposing Jean-Jacques Rousseau's *Letter to D'Alembert*." She smiled while we stared blankly at her. None of us had ever heard of the book. But somehow we guessed that the proposal was ridiculous — some sort of eighteenth-century essays like we'd had to read in college. Trying to emulate Cinder's professorial presence, Barbara sat up straight. She took a long sip of wine before placing her glass carefully down in front of her. Then she began reading her notes.

"The book argues that art is bad for us. Well, not exactly. It's more complicated. Rousseau says that art is bad for good people and good for bad people. Isn't that clever? Books have different effects on different people, depending on what they're already like. Plus Rousseau argues that art destroys morals. Rousseau says that women are naturally vain, but it's not their fault. They are doomed to worry about how they look because it's their nature. Living in cities makes them even more vain than they are naturally. He also argues that men wouldn't stay with women if women hadn't invented love to make them stay. Without that invented love, men would desert them to have sex with as many other women as possible. We'd need at most two reading sessions to talk about it."

Barbara smiled broadly, satisfied with her pitch. She took another long, slow sip of her wine. Olive, who had been making circles around the rim of her wine glass with her index finger, put both hands in her lap and cleared her throat. "I know this is breaking the rules, and I should ask a question and not comment, but too bad. I don't know this book, Barbara, but I didn't spend my youth marching in the streets on behalf of women's rights to end up reading this kind of crap."

Olive leaned forward across the table and pointed her finger directly at Barbara. "I fought for equal pay for equal work, for the right for women to have good jobs, for their right to birth control, for abortion rights, for all the stuff your generation of women take for granted." She was hissing, barely able to control her anger. "And now you come along and ask me to read this drivel?"

No one spoke a word. We'd been having occasional rows during the last several months, but no one had sounded as angry as this. Olive was always so calm and collected, so tolerant of any idea, no matter how stupid. We turned our heads to Annie, whom we always counted on to smooth things over. Annie tilted her head back, swigging down the last few drops of her wine. She then pointed to the empty bottle on the table. The waiter nodded knowingly and hustled off for another.

"Olive, dear," she said calmly, looking around the table, "it's not nice to break the rules. But now that you've gone and done it, permit me to respond."

Annie looked at Olive. "I think you're overreacting. We're all smart women here, and there's no reason to fear taking on a diatribe by a maniac like Rousseau. I haven't read the thing, but . . ." Annie paused, gazing down into her empty glass before turning directly to Barbara. "Frankly, I'm a little surprised by your choice, Barbara. Anyone with half a brain knows Rousseau is an unrepentant misogynist."

Like the rest of us, Barbara sought Annie's approval, so it was no surprise that she was devastated. Nancy rushed to join in. "Well, I may be a mere medical doctor, but I happen to know about Rousseau from college. Barbara, darling, don't take it personally. The guy was a nut case. His idea that man is basically good—the noble savage thing and all that? He knew diddly about human nature."

Nancy then softened her tone: "But let's not argue. Barbara's made her pitch."

Barbara filled her glass to the brim and said: "I don't appreciate people violating the rules by commenting instead of asking questions. Nor do I appreciate the attitude here. We say we're open-minded, but it turns out you're as close-minded as a bunch of small-town harridans. You're afraid of reading a little essay by a long-ago philosopher!" She then reached for the waiter's arm, surprising him by grabbing the wine bottle out of his hand.

"Well, the problem is, Barbara, maybe what everyone is saying is true," said Cinder, holding out her glass for a refill as well. "Sometimes the choices here aren't that great." She took a longish sip from her freshly filled glass and said: "But the important thing is that you're absolutely right that we're violating the rules here. So let's move on. We have *Rousseau's Letter to Whatever* as our first proposal. Laurie, it's your turn."

Laurie

There was nothing for me to do other than admit the truth, which is that I'd been too swamped with work to prepare a pitch. "I'm so sorry," I said. If looks were arrows, I'd have rivaled Saint Sebastian himself. No one smiled, not even Annie. Nancy, thankfully, stepped in once again. She took a big gulp of wine and immediately cut me off, plunging into her pitch, talking in that way of hers as if we were her patients.

Nancy

"Well, despite my busy practice, I've got a pitch." She put on her reading glasses and looked down at her notes. "Some of you will think this is self-serving, but I assure you, it's not." She took a sip of her wine before going on. "I'm proposing we read my book—the one I finished writing a few years back—*The*

Wondrous Hymen. As you know, I haven't yet found a publisher, but it's a damn lively book."

Annie raised her hand. "Hold it, hold it, hold it right there," she said, gesturing sloppily. "If this is your way to get me to show your manuscript to my editor, it's totally chicken. I've already told you that the subject of hymens bores me to tears, and I'm not interested in promoting your book to anyone."

Nancy calmly answered, "Annie, I'm sorry to be the one to inform you of this, but by interrupting me, you are violating the rules of our group." She then gave a disquisition on what the hymen is, how widely hymens vary, and why, even though they might appear useless, hymens occur in a lot of mammals. "The question for evolutionary biologists, then, is why they're there at all."

Nancy was clearly excited by her topic. "Medically speaking, the hymen is not a vestigial thing, like, say, your pinkie," she said, wiggling the little finger of her right hand. "My book addresses the large, unanswered question of why human females possess hymens."

"The reason is obvious," Annie said, violating the rules yet again while letting a little wine dribble down the front of her blouse. "The hymen is there to be broken!" With that, she picked up a piece of pita bread and poked her finger through its center.

"Actually, Nancy's book sounds worth reading," I said meekly. True, I was breaking the rules, but everyone else was too, so why not me? "I have no idea why the stupid hymen exists. I mean, maybe it's there for the man to know a woman is a virgin. How else would he know? Take the woman's word for it?" I asked, laughing at the suggestion.

Barbara, who had been pouting ever since she gave her pitch for Rousseau, chimed in. "First of all, hymens are easily able to be reconstructed. Second, they break all the time, even without sex. They don't prove a damn thing. But aside from all that, if we're willing to consider a book on the hymen, I don't see why we aren't willing to consider Rousseau."

Barbara took another sip of wine, put the glass down on the table, and argued her case once again. "Rousseau's actually talking about the same thing as the hymen problem — how nature made women different from men, and how this causes them to behave differently. To Rousseau, being modest is not some old-fashioned thing taught to us by our mothers, or pushed on us by patriarchal society. It's no 'social construct,' as Cinder likes to say. Female modesty is a natural thing. It's nature's way of preventing women from getting raped by out-of-control, testosterone-driven males."

Cinder

"Please. Everybody. You're all seriously breaking the rules. And enough of this hymen and Rousseau business. It's really perverse. I've got my own proposal here." She took a large swallow of wine and said, "I propose we read *Moby-Dick*."

"*Moby-Dick*," Nancy said, "is a boy's book."

"That's absolutely not true," Cinder declared. "Granted, there are no women in *Moby-Dick*, but this is precisely why it's perfect for us. We can talk about *ideas*, and the problem of the sexes in the *abstract*, without letting the problem of men get in the way. *Moby-Dick* is a postmodern discourse about the boundlessness of knowledge and the futility of the Western attempt to conquer nature. It covers the entire sum of knowledge, from homosexuality to the history of whaling, to capitalism, power, and psychosis, not to mention the meaning of the color white. There's a hell of a lot for us to talk about."

Olive leaned back while she poured herself yet another glass of wine. "Well, the important question is whether or not whales have hymens." That made everyone — even Barbara — slap the table in laughter.

"I had to read the book in high school — in the days when we were taught 'Great Books,'" Olive said. "I also saw the movie — the one with Gregory Peck. The movie is okay, but the book is a drag. It ends badly for Ahab and his crew, and I think anyone with half a mind sides with the whale."

Phoebe, who had quietly slipped into a chair at the beginning of Nancy's talk, hadn't said a word. But now she spoke up. "What happened before I got here? Did we change the rules about talking during pitches?"

Annie answered, "No, Phoebe. The rules haven't changed. Cinder just finished pitching *Moby-Dick*, and now it's Olive's turn."

Olive

"I'm pitching Marcus Aurelius's *Meditations*," Olive said immediately, with half a smile. "If you remember your Gibbon, Marcus Aurelius was one of the 'good' Roman emperors. This would be especially pleasurable for me now that I'm entering that phase of my life where it's natural to want to ruminate on life as a whole. We're talking second century AD. Marcus is a Stoic, of course—you can hardly have 'meditations' if you're not one. All striving in life is futile, and everyone needs to prepare for disaster and death. But I find him uplifting. He persecuted Christians, but he's got a dash of Christian compassion to his thinking."

"That's truly the weirdest suggestion I've ever listened to," Cinder said, breaking the silence. "Why not just go straight to the book of Job?"

Olive calmly answered: "Because I happen to be proposing *this* book, Cinder, and *not* the book of Job. That's why."

Annie folded and unfolded her hands before saying, "For some reason, all the proposals tonight are extra serious and less fun than anything we've done up to this point." She sat up straight and pushed back her hair before taking another sip of wine. Then she pulled out a note card from her purse.

"Okay, my turn. I propose we read the Marquis de Sade's *Philosophy in the Bedroom*. It's filthy and disgusting, full of terrible sex scenes that include torture, and doesn't have a single redeeming feature to it. Some feminists and postwhatevers interpret Sade as celebrating absolute freedom, but that's all poppycock. He's strictly a pervert, with special hatred directed at women and the church, which is where all the fun will be. I predict he'll have us laughing. What do you say?"

Barbara leaned forward on her elbows before placing her hands down on the table. "But," she said, slurring her words and spreading her fingers wide apart, "if the book is filthy and disgusting, like you say, Rousseau would say that it's going to harm those of us who are good. And that happens to include me. And those in the group who are bad (and most of you are bad) — those who are already inclined toward this Sade sort of gross stuff— will find they get even more bad. Or something like that."

"Barbara, you're talking nonsense," Olive said, patting her hand. "Who in the group is good? Who is bad? You'd better not have any more wine." With that, Olive pulled the bottle away so Barbara couldn't reach it, pouring some wine for herself instead.

Phoebe

"Annie," Phoebe said, "I believe you are sincere in offering this book by the Marquis de Sade, and in thinking we'd end up stronger by confronting sadomasochism. And I don't share Barbara's worries. We'd survive reading it. But what's the point? Why should we subject ourselves to horrible ideas? Even I, the youngest in the group, already know the world is full of terrible things. But with life so short, shouldn't we choose to dwell on what's good and beautiful instead of what's bad and ugly? I thought we all believed that reading books and talking about them over a glass of wine makes us *happier*. If it doesn't do that, what's the point of all of this?"

Phoebe then pulled out her own note card. "I've been thinking of proposing this for a long time. Let's read *Pride and Prejudice*."

All of us except Annie burst out laughing. Olive actually doubled over and managed to knock over some wine. Phoebe wasn't the least bit ruffled.

"Here's how I see it," she said, once everyone had calmed down. "You're older than I am, and like me, have already read this book. But none of us, including me, have *read* it — as in, read it with care. You think it's a book about clever, sparkling dialogue. And it is. But it's also about more than that. It's about how the union of Elizabeth Bennet and Darcy is not really possible and exists only in the imagination. That's why Austen doesn't follow them past their marriage — follow them to Pemberley after they have children. She knows the dark, unspeakable tragedy of the sexes — that men and women are ill-suited for one another and neither sex can find happiness in the other. Women, in struggling for survival, will always go for powerful men. They'll always fall for men they think are like Darcy. Men will always long for youth, beauty, and sex. Once Elizabeth starts to grow old, Darcy will start going to London once a week to indulge his libertine side. Bourgeois marriage is good for society and for raising children, but it doesn't offer happiness."

Annie looked at Phoebe and smiled wistfully. "You sound awfully disillusioned for someone so young, Phoebe. Look, Austen writes brilliant dialogue, but you can't turn her into a philosopher, or try to argue she's against marriage. Madame de Staël had it right: Austen's *vulgaire*. If we choose this book, we'll fall asleep."

Olive, feeling sorry for Phoebe, said: "Phoebe, I too love this book, but no one in it works for a living! I'll read it again only when Darcy gets a job."

"You're right," Phoebe said abruptly. "Darcy is ridiculous. He'd rather live his life alone than spend it with a woman who bores him. Men like Darcy don't exist."

Sarah

Suddenly, Sarah and a few of her friends arrived, sashaying over to our table. "I'm so, so absolutely sorry! Did I miss the pitches? I've got mine ready, please, please let me make it!" She waved her notes out in front of her. How beautiful she looked — dressed as if she were a goddess from on high.

"How could we ever turn down our darling Sarah?" asked Annie. "Go, girl. Make your pitch."

Sarah motioned to her friends to sit at another table. She sat down, squeezing herself next to Phoebe, whom she hugged. "I heard everything you said about Jane Austen, Phoebe, but we need to read something from the present." Sarah poured some wine into Phoebe's glass and then took a long drink straight from the bottle, letting a few shiny drops of wine run delicately down her chin.

"I propose we read Junot Díaz's *The Brief Wondrous Life of Oscar Wao*. Everyone on the subway is reading it. It'll make a fab discussion, and it gets us away from bickering about the sexes. The author is a Dominican American who writes about the people in the Dominican Republic and how they all come from a mix of all the races and continents. It's the past, present, and future all rolled into one."

"What's wrong?" Sarah asked, when everyone at the table sat in stunned silence. "Did I do something wrong?" Then she sounded sharper. "Is my pitch too hip and contemporary for this group of ladies?"

"No, Sarah, that's not it." Annie was pronouncing each word slowly, and with care. "It's just that . . . well, what can I say? You've somehow pitched a book that hasn't been published yet, and won't even be written for another fifteen years. It doesn't exist yet."

We'd had a lot of wine — perhaps we were drunk. Grasping this idea was too perplexing for anyone to handle.

Sarah whimpered. "But it's out there. I've *heard* about it."

"No you haven't. But who cares? Let's just vote. We need to go home and sober up," Olive said.

We made our ballots and tossed them into the center of the table. Olive counted the votes — seven abstentions and one vote for *Pride and Prejudice*.

"So who voted for *Pride and Prejudice*?" Sarah asked, puzzled.

"It doesn't matter," Annie said, gathering her purse and sweater as she rose from the table. "I'm sorry, but this is it, at least for me. Good luck, everybody."

With that, Annie walked away from the table and left the restaurant. The rest of us left shortly afterward, never to meet as a group again.

▼ Imbibing as a Lady

*M*rs. Geiger was a different kind of mom but a mom all the same. Passing around the bong, she'd scold us to "Hold it in! Don't waste!" even as we rolled around hacking on the Marimekko print sofa. It was okay to be wasted but not *wasteful*. This was an important distinction if you wanted to hang out in Mrs. Geiger's house.

Of course we all did, endlessly. Suzanne Geiger had the whole basement to herself—refrigerator, TV and Betamax, and a separate door to the outside. Caught breaking curfew, high, drunk, with a boy, or even all four at once, and the worst Suzanne Geiger suffered was a lecture over homemade Linzer torte: it's better to party at home than out God knows where . . .

This was Queens circa 1980. None of my other tennis team pals even remotely shared this philosophy. If Sunday morning often found me, hungover, vacuuming pot seeds and Dorito crumbs off the basement rug while Mrs. Geiger stood by glaring from under her blond bob, I still could not believe my luck. And with a thorough cleanup came coffee.

At seventeen, I found even coffee drinking *chez* Geiger exotic. They ground the beans themselves, used a French press, and drank from hand-thrown mugs. There was always a tablecloth. There was never cursing, bad grammar, or gossip. These habits Mrs. Geiger deemed "crude and common," along with wearing bright red lipstick, exposing oneself to sexual diseases, and drinking alcohol, especially cheap alcohol out of a bottle or can.

"So you can't afford Heineken every day? Is that some reason not to imbibe as a lady?"

I still have a vision of her espadrilles and perfect posture as she descends the stairs bearing a tray of flowered drinking glasses.

Mrs. Geiger was Swiss, which to me explained everything. (That and the fact that the rarely present Mr. Geiger was an introverted undertaker with long hair and a leather vest.) The family dined at 8:00 by candlelight, and teens were allowed to drink wine with the meal, even on school nights. Sometimes that meal was salad. Salad as a meal! The idea alone got me buzzed. This was a salad of fresh greens, unlike the hunks of iceberg lettuce served at my house. Good bread, too, with grains in it, and cheese — cheese! — for dessert.

In contrast, my home seemed comically straight. What we called supper was served at 6:00 on plastic Disney placemats. If a friend was eating over, we ran upstairs to warn Dad so he wouldn't come down to dinner in his underwear. We washed the iceberg lettuce, daily meat, and starch down with Coke.

My parents weren't teetotalers, just Jews. They didn't exactly know how to drink. Finding herself in a cocktail situation, my mother would order Kahlua and coffee and, a few sips in, start exclaiming, "Wooo, I feel a little . . ." as she wiggled her fingers by the side of her head. Still, they were fun people who liked to entertain. For these occasions, they trained my brother to wheel out a little table and create Café Don Juan — a flaming rum concoction that they'd had on some long-ago Puerto Rican vacation. But the fine wines and brandies that guests brought as gifts were taken to the laundry room and quickly forgotten.

By them, that is. My friends and I sure remembered. We didn't even have to water down the bottles. When we weren't at the Geigers', we lay around on my lime-green bedspread quaffing champagne out of tennis ball cans and comparing moms.

"Stop at one drink or else!" Camille's mother would call after her, never once following up on the threat.

Allie's mom was less concerned with inebriation than calories. "You don't realize how fattening! At least make it a spritzer."

My own mother hadn't a clue what I was up to, or else she was in complete denial.

Which left Mrs. Geiger. She alone had our trust, and not because she smoked pot with us, which is the way I would have explained it back then. Not because she worked (for some Swiss company), either, or played folk guitar. It was simply that she was the only one really watching, the only one offering guidance, however unorthodox.

As Suzanne's eighteenth birthday neared, she nixed our plans for a monster keg party.

"A keg party? Haven't I taught you girls anything?" But if we were willing to celebrate properly—cook some real food, use utensils, and decorate—she'd fund a case of Heineken.

A kitchen fire, a lopsided seven-layer cake, and many toasts to the legal drinking age later, I awoke on the Marimekko upholstery to hear Suzanne saying, "I don't know. Jill brought it."

Nearby, Mrs. Geiger knelt over the long-emptied bottle I had swiped from my laundry room as a gift.

"Have you any idea"—she was croaking, squeezing her head —"what this costs? What this is?"

"Good wine?" I guessed.

"When your parents find out . . ."

I nodded. It seemed disrespectful to everyone involved to mention that my parents would never notice, could not tell a great vintage from swill.

"I wish I could have tasted it," said Mrs. Geiger, her voice so full of longing that I was afraid she might cry. "What was it like, you guys? Tell me."

We hung our heads awhile until Suzanne finally thought to lie: "It was delicious, Mom!"

The rest of us followed suit.

"Dry dry."

"Awesome."

Camille, whose dad liked wine, even managed: "Complex."

I wanted badly to see the label then, but Mrs. Geiger was already floating up the stairs, holding the bottle aloft like a lantern. Grabbing the vacuum, I got busy on the rug and vowed to start paying attention right then, forever.

Now I have my own teenage daughters and my own additions to the "crude and common" file: anonymous Facebook posts, cigarettes, thong underwear sticking up from the back of your jeans. I'm not exactly Mrs. Geiger when it comes to house rules, but sips of my wine at dinners are fine, especially if my daughters note how it tastes. Because luckily I married a man with the last name of Drinkard, so spell check keeps asking them: "Do you mean Drunkard?" And they are adamant, at least so far, that they absolutely don't.

▼ The Drink

I have pretty much given up the idea that I will ever enjoy The Drink.

That's wine, beer, liquor, and frou-frou mixed drinks — all of it regretfully poured down the drain to swirl off in an amber flow to the party down the street, where perhaps people dwell who would enjoy it.

I will never stumble into a drinking establishments and, floozy-like, throw my breasts over the bar to order a tall one. I will never sit with the snots or swells discussing the grape or the grain with any degree of grace, nor will I ever — most likely — learn to open wine in such a way that the drinker next to me won't feel compelled to take the instrument out of my hands before I cut myself or stab through the bottle.

Blame Jesus for my current sober state. I do.

I grew up in a fundamentalist Christian church that forbade drinking because the quickest way to be induced to remove one's panties unduly was to

1 Dance and
2 Drink.

And once the kids in my youth group learned just how much fun was sex, we'd never warm a pew again. And then Jesus would return and find us wanting, and we would be placed with the rest of the chaff, the sinners who go to hell where our flesh would melt from our bones throughout all eternity.

You could look it up. We did. It's in there.

That's the boiled-down version of the theology that caught in my net, and though the original message was probably more nuanced, the shadings went right by me. During one high-school football game, the rumor spread that Terry, a friend of mine, was drinking beneath the stands. I went to retrieve her and cried over her lost state.

For her part, Terry was gracious enough not to tell me to mind my own business, though she would have been well within her rights to do so. I don't believe our friendship ever quite recovered, and why would it? Not drinking cut me off from countless house parties when someone's parents would just be pulling around the corner for a nice daylong fishing trip and my classmates, like locusts, would descend with six-packs galore. I didn't get the phone call to show up in the chat piles (piles of radioactive gravel left over from my hometown's old mining days) because who wants to throw a party and invite a grind—or, worse, a fundamentalist who'll bring along her Bible to swing like Carry Nation's hatchet?

I did not grow up drinking, and while it is a talent one can acquire later—like piano playing—there's always just a bit of a paucity of talent. You can practice and practice, but you'll never make the travel team unless you start young.

Beyond the theology, we were frightened away from the bottle by a thick vein of alcoholism that runs through my family. We knew which uncle and which grandfather had pickled themselves to death. In our fundamentalist home, drinkers were looked on with much disdain, and if I had opened up the refrigerator and found a wine bottle there, I would have hurried outside because I would have known I had wandered into the wrong house. We. Didn't. Drink.

So while sex and sin were to be had all around me (this being the 1970s), I rounded up my sober loser buddies to try to have fun anyway. Someone would grab their mother's car, and we would go vandalize the homes of private citizens. I believe we were trying to prove to our drinking friends that we could be just as wild and crazy, even without the encouragement of alcohol.

There was a hollowness to it, but I think I was having fun without alcohol. If my friends were boring, they weren't scary, and I could relax around them even while I felt a longing to be in the cool crowd. Still, I had the added incentive of my teachers' love to keep me on the straight and narrow. My teachers would compliment me on my clean lifestyle. That I was out drag-racing and beating in mailboxes with bats and executing general mayhem was rarely held against me because at least I wasn't drinking. It was Good Clean Fun. I was a Good Kid, and that gave me a lot of leeway into deviant behavior.

I certainly could have loosened up in college, far from the eyes of my hometown. My dorm room was right next to the lobby where everyone gathered to drink from Friday afternoon until Monday's wee hours. I managed to figure out how to have sex without the alcohol (the chaser without the drink), and I continued my career in vandalizing, but I remained the pet of my professors because I never showed up for class red-eyed and silly.

Still. These were my friends partying. During the keg parties, I stayed in my room and felt like a hypocrite. I no longer worried about being an alcoholic—I'd tasted wine at a friend's Passover seder and hated it—but I'd grown so accustomed to avoiding it entirely that that's all I knew to do. My friends tried to get me to at least come out in the hall. I didn't. I didn't feel particularly righteous, but I could no more walk into a keg party than I could walk into fire—which still felt like the same thing. If I lost control, who would I be? If the boys around me lost control, where would I be?

After college, and fully in control of myself and the world, I began trying to redeem myself. I am a journalist. We. Drink. So with an eye on serious research, for years I sought an alcoholic beverage that I could like. There's something about the image of a dame like me sauntering into some dive, throwing my arms over the bar and demanding a Jack Daniel that appeals to me. I longed for an easy and happy relationship with alcohol, one I could come back to whenever I chose and not worry about maintaining.

With lockjaw sincerity, I sucked down margaritas, knocked back sea breezes, gagged on tequila, sipped wine (and poured the bulk of it into nearby plants), and chugged beer that always tasted like rotten apples. I once won a bottle of whiskey in a raffle, took it home, and tried that, too. It burned all the way down. That was Christmas of '92, and only in my last move did I finally pour it out in the yard.

Still, a few times I would drink just enough to achieve that lovely buzz, when everyone's funny and happy and kind, when I am beautiful and so is the world. And then I'd have one more sip and things would turn to shit.

Friends would insist that I needed to loosen up, but even I could detect the smarminess when I took two sips from a drink and then excitedly turned to the person with me and asked, "Am I drunk? Do I sound drunk?"

No. I sound . . . something—but emphatically not drunk.

I now know why I didn't drink in the bloom of my immaturity. I am a cheap drunk. I read labels, and my eyes start to roll. Two drinks, and I'm talking louder than necessary. Only once did I actually drink so much that the room spun and I had to lie down. When I woke up the next morning, I felt like a cat had fallen asleep in my mouth. Perhaps one had. I was too frightened to check.

And perhaps Jesus was looking out for me, after all. If I had been a drinker in high school, I would have gone home with the first guy who asked, borne three or four woods colts (that's what we called children born outside of wedlock then), and ended up for life in a trailer just outside of town. That's all from that first sip of Bud. I'm pretty sure I'm right.

Although I'm never that far from that trailer, I no longer fear the future and my place in it. I am beyond the woods-colt stage, but it's still a little embarrassing to be this old and not have a drink I can order with assurance. Bars still make me nervous. When I go into one, I am awed by the labels and fancy bottles. And I am still—naively—struck with the evilness of it all. Oooh, we're *drinking*. Except I lack some inhibitions that float to the top of the bottle the deeper you dive. I don't need the help.

My husband handles this better than I do. He is a social drinker who knows his limits. He has described his imbibing thus: One beer, and he's witty. Two beers, he's rambunctious. Three beers, he's awfully quiet. Four beers, he's waking up in his own vomit. It is a progression I understand, though I generally can cut out the two middle beers.

Still. At my age, when I order a diet Coke ("Just a Coke," I apologize to the waiter), they look at me funny, like maybe I had a problem with drinking, and now I'm just working my program. I'm about at the point where I want to say: "Well, I have had a problem with drinking, and this is my program."

So at the next barbeque/rent party/shindig, when the liquor flows like . . . liquor, I will order a Coke or a Dr Pepper, if they have it. And when I get the sympathetic looks, I will quote Pete Hamill and say that I simply have no talent for drinking. I will, however, sit back and admire the people who do.

And I will leave it at that.

▼ Drink and the Single Girl

*m*y parents spent a long time picking names for my sister and me. Their main criteria were that the names be traditional Gaelic ones and that they couldn't be shortened or "butchered." I got Niamh (Neeve), and my sister got Orlaith (Or-la). Niamh was the princess of Tír na nÓg (the Land of Eternal Youth) in Gaelic mythology, and Orlaith means "golden lady." It seems only natural, then, that as a child, I had a princess complex. I would dress up in my mom's nightgowns and high heels and pretend I was a real princess. I was short enough that the dresses reached the floor, and my patient mother would put pretty clips in my hair to hold it back. My dad grew flowers in our front garden, and I would pick as many as I could to fill my hand, since I was convinced that every princess needs a bouquet of flowers. My dad wasn't impressed that I was picking his precious Sweet Williams, but I think the very sight of me walking from the front yard to the playhouse that he built for me was enough to make him laugh rather than make him cross—my ability to walk in high heels has improved only slightly since then.

It also seemed only natural that when I came of age, I used aliases in bars because for some reason, people (men) just couldn't understand "Niamh." They would hear meeve, leave, Steve. Anything except Niamh. And God help me if they heard it correctly and then wanted to know how to spell it. I worked through a few aliases before settling on Kate. It was short and easy to hear, and since my middle name is Catherine, Dad has always called me Kate. Gertrude-but-my-friends-call-me-Trudy got me a date at a bar. I was in the Hamptons celebrating a friend's birthday, and it was the first time I tried Gertrude. I told my friends the plan, and they remembered to call me Trudy. He introduced himself with a horrible pick-up line. (He overheard us talking about running and asked us if we had ever been to the Penn Relays in November (the Penn Relays take place in April, but I must have felt pity and overlooked this).

We danced until closing time, and as the night went on, I began to imagine our matching embroidered towels and a Hamptons wedding. When he asked me for my number, I grabbed his phone and started entering it myself, but then the phone wanted me to enter my name. After a few rum and Cokes, I had no idea which fake name I had given him. Gertrude? Mildred? Kate? So I asked him, trying to make it sound as flirtatious as possible. Apparently I was going for multiple personalities that night, since his answer was that my name was Gertrude but I hated it so I let my friends call me Trudy and I tell people my name is Kate. I typed Kate into the phone, gave him one more kiss, and hoped for the best.

He called while I was at work on Monday and left a message: "Hey, Kate. It's Michael from Saturday night. Just calling to see how you are. Give me a call when you get a chance."

What was I supposed to do? I knew I had a confession to make, so I called him on my way home.

NIAMH: Hey. So I have small, very small, minute confession to make.

MICHAEL: Umm, okay. What is it?

NIAMH: Well, my name isn't Kate.

MICHAEL: I know. It's Gertrude. You let your friends call you Trudy.

NIAMH: Well, that's not true either. It's Niamh. I hate giving my real name at bars because it's hard to explain when music is blasting.

MICHAEL: It's what?

NIAMH: It's Niamh. Like "Eve" with an *n* at the beginning.

MICHAEL: Oh. Niamh. I get it. So why did you not want to give your real name?

NIAMH: Well, how many Niamhs have you met? You could be some psycho stalker for all I know.

MICHAEL: But you gave me your real number! Promise your real name is Niamh?

NIAMH: Yes, I promise.

We went on one mediocre date in New York, and the rest is history.

My parents had better luck, but their first meeting left a little to be desired. They met in a pub in Lourdes, France, two young lovebirds who had a date with kismet. They were there to do God's work through the Knights of Malta, and God knows the spirits were flowing. She, the petite beauty with the quick tongue from the center of Ireland, arrived at the pub with the mutual friend to meet "a real character." He, the handsome blue-eyed joker from the northwest, was holding court when the other two arrived. Unfortunately, there wasn't a good moment for the prospective couple to meet, but she had seen enough to venture with the friend to the joker's hotel the next day for a proper introduction. Little did they know that the joker was waiting at his hotel window with a bucket full of water. He poured it at what he thought was the right time in an attempt to get the friend, but he missed entirely and soaked the beauty.

And so began the story of my parents, Anne (née Marsh) and Paddy Cunningham. They started dating officially soon after this incident (who wouldn't?), broke up a couple of times (what love story doesn't have some good breakups?), and eventually got engaged. A unique aspect of their courtship was that for much of it, my dad was studying in England. They wrote each other letters (real letters, not e-mail; he to his "Dearest Annie" and she to her "Darling Paddy") and talked on the phone when they could, though that wasn't often. When my dad asked my grandfather if he could marry my mom, my grandfather said, "You can, of course, if you can live with her," both knowing that my mom and my grandmother were in the kitchen laughing at the two of them.

My parents have been married for over twenty-five years, and they're still going strong. She still has her quick tongue, and he's still a joker. I called home one Valentine's Day on my way into Manhattan, and Mom answered the phone. I could hear in the background, "Who's that calling the house on Valentine's Day?"

"It's your eldest child," my mother said.

"Doesn't she know we're watching *Jeopardy*?" Dad said.

"Watching *Jeopardy*?" I asked. "Is that what the kids are calling it these days?"

"Ha. Joke's on you, Niamh," Mom said. "Your father just missed Final Jeopardy, and you know how much he loves getting the answer to that one."

Dad, unwilling to let the joke drop, said, "Would you tell her to leave us alone and call back in about fifteen minutes?"

I certainly hope that I'm still able to make jokes like that when I've been married for twenty-five years. I should probably say *if* I'm married for twenty-five years; saying "when" sounds so presumptuous, and what single girl ever wants to sound presumptuous? It's unbecoming. Besides, I'm hardly going to be setting a wedding date any time soon if I'm not even scheduling first dates. Though can you blame me after my last first date? Tell me a story about a bad first date, and I'm pretty sure I can tell you a story about a worse one. After this latest debacle, I've been keeping my calendar free of all dates, no matter what the occasion.

It all started about when my co-worker asked me if it would be okay for her to give my e-mail address to an old friend of hers. My co-worker and I are good friends, and I trusted her. She said he was nice, funny, smart, thirty-two, and looked like Pete Sampras. She had barely said, "Pete Sam-" before I said, "Yes!" I wasn't desperate; I've just always thought Pete Sampras was hot.

A few days after my co-worker and I talked, her friend e-mailed me, and he seemed like a nice guy. He had a joke right in the first sentence, so he was starting off well. The e-mails went back and forth for a while before he finally asked me on a date. I was booked solid that Friday and Saturday, so I asked if Sunday was okay. I figured a Sunday lunch would be a good first meeting. He went one step further and suggested a movie followed by dinner. He'd be at my place at ten of 4:00.

I spent Sunday recovering from a slight hangover and cleaning my apartment. He arrived at my door ten minutes early. He was no Pete Sampras, and he barely resembled the picture he'd sent me in one of his e-mails. The guy looking at me was bald and had sprouted facial hair. Needless to say, the awkward go-in-for-the-hug-but-change-my-mind moment lasted an eternity. I gave him a brief tour of my apartment, stalling in an attempt to think of an excuse to get out of going to the movie. It wasn't that he was bald—I've got nothing against bald people. Really. I just don't like bald liars.

I couldn't think of anything quick enough, so we got into the car and made our way to the theater. On the way there, we attempted small talk. At one point there was a pause, and he declared, completely out of the blue, "I don't really like sports. I never really follow them. I do like boxing, though."

Boxing? Really? I was so screwed. And not in the good way. In a freak reversal of roles, it was nerd meets jock, and I was the jock.

We finally made it to our seats at the movie, and I thought the previews would never start. The conversation was painful, and since it was the 4:20 showing of *Marley and Me*, the theater started to fill up with geriatrics who probably used their senior citizen discounts on the matinee tickets. He asked me (again, out of the blue), "Are you a risk taker?"

I said: "I don't mull things over when making decisions. I don't spend hours or days weighing all of the options and doing tons of research. I listen to my gut, know what I want, and go for it, so I guess in some respects that would be considered a risk taker."

"I like to plan," he said. "I spend a lot of time thinking about the options and it takes me a while to reach a decision." Guess that explains why it took forever for him to ask me out.

I was so angry at my date for lying and for being so horrible at having a conversation that I couldn't even cry when Marley died. I'm the girl who cries at Hallmark commercials, and I couldn't even shed a tear when the poor dog died? Sure enough, when I watched the movie again without my date, I sobbed my eyes out.

When we got to the restaurant, I said a little prayer to Saint Jude for an efficient waitress. It worked, and our waitress came over right away. While we were waiting for our food, we made more attempts at bad small talk, but I was even less inclined to participate than I had been in the theater. Somehow I managed to get through dinner with just a lemonade (he had a soda), and by the time we were done, I had had enough. When the check came, I insisted he let me help, hoping it would speed up our exit. The drive home was longer than I wanted it to be, and on the way there, he opened a pack of gum, took a piece for himself, and offered me one. I had seen this move before (and used it myself once or twice), but I had no intention of kissing him at the door, so I declined. It was all I could do not to sprint out of the car and up my steps, but I stayed long enough to thank him for a nice time and to wish him a good night.

When I got up to my apartment, I dropped my bag on my table and said out loud, "Pete Sampras my ass!"

I called my sister and walked over to her place. She had dessert and a big glass of wine waiting for me and promptly got a pain in her side from laughing so hard at my sad tale.

My love life wasn't always full of such sad tales. In college I dated a guy whom I thought I would marry. For all intents and purposes, we got engaged just before my twentieth birthday. But in all honesty, what girl would say no to her first love when he gets down on one knee and proposes (sans diamond) when they're standing on top of a landfill and covered in sweat because they're in the middle of a run? I certainly didn't. From then on, we spent the rest of the relationship planning the rest of our lives. We were those kids in the college dining hall who exchanged knowing glances with each other whenever a Huggies commercial came on the television as we both envisioned our future family.

One of my girlfriends sat next to me during a class, and when the lights dimmed in the auditorium, we would plan our weddings to our respective boyfriends. We had ideal dates picked out, and no detail went without discussion: What kind of flowers? Who would be in the bridal party? What would the color scheme be? Band or DJ? What would the first dance be? What would the father-daughter song be? Where would the wedding be? What season? Fancy dress or more casual? Bottled, plain, or sparkling? Soup or salad? Mashed, baked, or fried? Dressing?

I broke up with my boyfriend by my twenty-first birthday (in large part thanks to a semester studying under Gina. I thanked her for it after graduation, and I continue to be grateful to her years later). Reflection has made me realize that I wasn't suffering from heartache at the end of the relationship but heartburn — that sort of planning is nauseating.

My friend's planning didn't go for naught, however, as she did manage to find a groom and get hitched. My track record with men since my first beau was spotty at best, so I wasn't at all surprised to receive no "Plus One" card in the wedding invitation. The wedding was beautiful, so beautiful that it was featured in an issue of *The Connecticut Bride*, a testament to all of her planning. There was a cocktail hour before the reception started, complete with a special wedding martini. It was orange in color and fit in with the fall theme of the wedding. One of my friends and I tried it, but neither of us are big on pumpkin flavoring in our alcohol. We realized that not only would we have to ditch our almost-full drinks in plain sight, but we'd also have to go right back up to the bar and order something else. That was about the only time I was shy about going back up to the bar. I ordered my usual favorite, a glass of Pinot Grigio, and tipped the bartender, hoping that would somehow make him judge me less for my double order.

After that, I continued to mingle and chat with old friends. My college roommate was there, and we hadn't seen each other in a while, so we had a lot to catch up on. We allowed ourselves to lament our single status for only a bit, focusing instead on how beautiful our friend was and how happy she looked on her wedding day. I don't know about my roommate, but part of me was beginning to wonder if I really wanted to get married. I had had enough of bad dates and worrying if the next guy would be another teetotaler or if he could read. I went on a date that started off brilliantly (well, except for the fact that we had water instead of wine with dinner due to his "one too many" nights out in college) and ended with him telling me he divided books into two categories: books with big words and books with small words. His "middle ground," if you will, was books with small words on a difficult subject, like Buddhism. I hadn't used the terms "big words" and "small words" since the second grade, and I didn't quite understand what he meant. I picked up Leon Uris's *Trinity* and asked him to give me an example of a big word. He chose "bedlam." I chose to exit, stage right.

I probably would have settled for either a drinker or a reader, but who wants to settle? I could feel the bitterness and cynicism rising with each sip of wine. The sips turned to glasses, and by the time I got to my table and realized it was all singles, I was embracing my single status. I was three glasses in, and I decided I wasn't getting married. Why would I want to? I had the New York apartment that I had always wanted, I had great friends, I had a great job, and I didn't have some guy taking up all the blankets, drinking out of the milk carton, and leaving the toilet seat up. I was set, really.

I clapped for my friend as she and her new husband were introduced to the guests, and I cried a few Pinot Grigio–induced tears when they danced their first dance, knowing this was such a big dream of hers. But my mind was made up: no marriage for this girl.

And then it happened.

It happens at almost every wedding, and I should have seen it coming. All the single ladies were called to the dance floor for the Tossing of the Bouquet. Ugh. I knew I had to do it. The bride had already made the rounds, telling us we had to get out there, and no one says no to a bride on her wedding day no matter how much wine he or she has had. I stood with the other single ladies, but I was probably the only one who didn't want to catch the bouquet. My plan was to pretend to try to catch it. Otherwise I'd be the odd one out, as all the other women dove for the bouquet, and that would be a bit too obvious.

The first throw went way over our heads. We lined up again, ready to go, and the DJ gave the bride the go-ahead. The next thing I knew, the stupid bouquet was coming right at me. So I did the classy thing and batted it to the ground. I don't know if there is a video, but if there is, it probably caught the look of sheer panic on my face. Everyone knows the superstition that the woman who catches the bouquet is the next one to get married, and I had just made up my mind not to marry. This would ruin everything!

In the split second between my batting the bouquet and its reaching the floor, I got caught up in the moment. The Pinot that had worked so hard to get me to swear off marriage also made me bend over and pick up the bouquet. Besides, this was the bride's day, and it wasn't mine to announce my newest self-revelation. Everyone clapped, and I realized they were all looking at me. I ran over to the bride and hugged her, and we both started cracking up. Perpetually-single-but-never-without-a-story-about-a-bad-date-Niamh caught the bouquet at the wedding of the girl who had been planning it since the womb. There has to be a certain irony in that.

I celebrated with another glass of Pinot while I watched the garter toss. I managed to get through the part where the guy put the garter on me with minimal mortification, considering that the bride's parents were watching. I also had to dance with the guy in front of everyone, but I got through that, too. I rewarded myself with another glass of Pinot (notice a pattern?), and danced my heels off during the rest of the reception, only stopping to refill my glass. When the "So when *are* you getting married?" questions started coming my way, I found myself saying, "When I find him," or, "When he finds me," or, "When we find each other," clearly ignoring the resolution I had made only hours earlier. Looking back, my answers weren't that bad, especially the last one. You can't plan for love; you just have to go with it when you find it (or it finds you), and in the meantime, always make sure you have a chilled bottle of Pinot in reserve.

The next day, I started thinking about married life, clearly over my fleeting resolution, and I realized I'd make a pretty good 1950s housewife, my culinary skills notwithstanding. I know how to knit, sew, crochet, cross-stitch (both counted and stamped), and make a quiche, a good cup of tea, and a killer manhattan. I also know how to waltz and swing dance. Here's hoping that whoever the fortunate guy is, he enjoys his whiskey, and if I'm really lucky, he'll know the manhattan was Ring Lardner's drink of choice. A literate drinker? Send him my way!

I'll drink to that. *Sláinte!*

A

I've had so many hangovers —
my brain must have stretch marks.
I went to an Alcoholics Anonymous meeting. A.A.
If you know everybody there is it just A?

I'm not an alcoholic but I do have addictions.
I thought a twelve-step program would help
but I didn't want to be around people who were just like me.
Blechhh.
I did not want to have to look at myself.
So I went to an A.A. meeting instead.
I'm not even sure they have meetings for people with my
    affliction
but A.A. was close to my house and they had delicious coffee.

I'm addicted to ice cream.
I go to a thirty-one-step program.
I'm doing okay, but last week I had some shakes.

One day I get to a meeting early and I sit behind two strangers.
I hear them talking about me.
"She's a stand-up comedian."
Blah blah blah.
And then the guy says my name.
First AND last!

"Ahem!" I said.
"I thought this was supposed to be anonymous!"
The woman blushed,

took a sip of her delicious coffee.
The man hemmed and hawed,
then told me his name
first AND last!
trying to appease me and apologize.

I was furious!
How dare he reveal my identity!
But I was also really happy that someone knew who I was.

I'm always happy when somebody recognizes me.
Especially if it's my mother.

I went to A.A. for a while.
I listened to stories
from heart-wrenching to boring,
mind-blowing to depressing,
uplifting and unbelievable.
I could relate to a lot of it.

Scientists discovered the gene for alcoholism.
It was the one wearing a lampshade.

I've been DRUNK four times.
I don't mean karaoke drunk,
where you drink enough to sing *MacArthur Park*
in a lounge in Vegas at the top of your lungs off-key with your
    skirt hiked up.
I've done that.

I mean I've been DRUNK four times,
room-swirling
head-razing
hangover-inducing
liquor-consuming
with no holds barred, no bars passed, bottle-swigging-the-hard-
    stuff *wasted*!

These are light-bulb memories
(ironic because when you're hungover you want to be in the
    dark),
the kind of memories you recall vividly because of their
    significance,
their trauma,
their drama,
their juiciness.

1

The first time I got DRUNK was in high school.
I was with my friends Beth and Debbie.
We had just consumed the best onion rings on Long Island at
    the Landmark Diner,
and then proceeded to imbibe rum and Coke from highball
    glasses at one of our houses, until everything suddenly went
    Alice in Wonderland.
The three of us passed out on the white shag rug mat in the
    bathroom.
I still can't eat onion rings or even smell rum to this day.

2

After taping a special for HBO in San Francisco,
I managed to dance the night away,
drinking enough of whatever anyone was buying
to the point of obliterating the rest of the weekend.
WHAT WAS I THINKING?!

3

I had been blonde for a few years,
but I was having too much fun.
I wanted to dye it back to its original color, brown.
But the hair person made it black.
Like black black.
Shoe-polish black.

I looked like Morticia.
I downed enough Johnnie Walker 'til I blacked out like my hair.
(At some point I threw up in it.)

4

My husband and I drank martinis in Manhattan at the
    Mayflower Hotel.
It was like an episode of *Sex and the City* except the sex part is
    blurry.
The flashbulb in this memory was a strobe.

I'm addicted to the remote control.
"God, grant me the serenity to accept the things that I cannot
    change —
like the channel."

My favorite part of A.A. was at the end, when everyone held
    hands.
When I felt like I was a part of something bigger,
while still being an integral link in the chain.
If we were an element we would have been mercury.

Maybe not everyone has a problem.
But most of my friends are obsessed with or dependent on
    something,
have a bad habit or would like to change one of their self-
    destructive behaviors.

My hope is that one day there is a meeting called H.A.
Humans Anonymous.
Or H.A.H.A.
His and Hers Anonymous.
It would be run like traditional twelve-step programs,
but you wouldn't have to divulge your darkness.
You could just partake in the healing process that occurs
    naturally when people gather.
It would be strangers in a beautiful sunny comfortable room

Eating snacks, sharing stories, connecting.
Tears and flowers.
A candle, laughter.
Hope.
Light.
Collective grief and then relief.
Maybe easier sleep.

I used to drink but I gave it up for rent.

The thirst and the headache the next day.
Is that to shrink the head from the brain?
Twist the ego out through shame?
Defiance, pain, deflation. The change of breath?
Self-recrimination?

My soul surrenders. Brake pads all worn down now. Grinding
metal to the asphalt.

That was the last straw. The last drop.
I give up. I give in. I am done.

Now's another chance
to begin
again.

stephanie k. hopkins

▼ By Way of Booze and Broccoli
One Woman's Search for the
Great American Dream

*From up here, nothing of Argia can be seen; some say, "It's
down below there," and we can only believe them. The place
is deserted. At night, putting your ear to the ground, you can
sometimes hear a door slam.*

▼   Italo Calvino, *Invisible Cities*

Working did to the trouble what gin did to the pain.

▼   Joan Didion, *Slouching Towards Bethlehem*

W*est*
hen I think about bars, I think about my dad. And cows.
I think about my dad surrounded by cows. It's one of those tricks
of the mind, the way memory presses odd images together and
makes them inseparable. I see a glass of scotch—the peaty,
single-malt kind, like Laphroaig or Glenlivet, the kind that re-
quires, for those in the know, a certain subtle tightening of the
back of the throat to momentarily disengage the taste buds and
engage the sense of smell. It's one of my favorite party tricks:
teaching people how to nose scotch. And every time I do it—
every time I inhale the pungent fumes through my mouth, up
my throat, and into my nose—I see cows.

In my mind, they are brown and white and perfectly spot-
ted. They're chewing that sideways way that cows do. My dad
has woken up to the surprise of them. When he went to sleep
in his Westfalia van in the middle of the night, in the middle of
a field that seemed just a field, after a long, satisfying day of fly-
fishing, he thought he would wake up early enough to continue
his solitary journey west. He didn't expect cows, and he certainly

153

didn't expect so many of them. But there he is, in a sea of them, unable to open the van's doors or move even an inch.

The bar is not far from the field. Or it is very far. In this wide expanse, who can tell distances anymore? It waits for local men, promising ritual and regularity. It waits for outsiders like my dad, as well, offering the comfort of continuity — this could be any bar, with its weathered wood, its dim lighting, the gentle creak of an oak floor — alongside the adventure of the new.

Who is the man who enters the bar, backlit sun casting his face in shadow as he opens the door? Maybe he is someone's father, someone's husband. But today, he is as I see him, drawn from stories and a young girl's imagination: fearless explorer of the Wild West, New England schoolteacher turned cowboy, American hero, bovine king.

It is over scotch that he tells the story, and it is over beer and whiskey that strangers listen. There is a hush across the bar as he recounts the way he bumped each cow over and over — gently — with his fender for hours, until one by one they inched out of his way. You can hear glasses clink in the wake of the listening, maybe the low hum of sports on TV. Even the bartender leans in to hear this one. Most likely, there's a joke at the end of the story, not an elaborately plotted one, but a short pun: "And that is why it is best to not kowtow to one's fears . . ."

The man who walked into this bar, in a small town in a big state very far away from where he lives, who has spent the last few weeks traversing river and road without cell phone or GPS, is at once soft-spoken and commanding, kind to animals and people alike, though capable of throwing a punch if necessary. He is not afraid to travel alone, nor enter an unknown bar, nor abandon himself to a geography greater than him. He drinks scotch and weaves stories, and he is exactly the kind of man this adolescent girl wanted to be.

The Boys' Club

Don Draper, self-made advertising man from *Mad Men* (Matthew Weiner's series about 1960s Madison Avenue advertising executives and the women who love them, bed them, and try to be them), sips scotch at his desk to celebrate a new account. The others from Accounting and Creative join him, and they all make a toast to themselves. As they joke and congratulate themselves, Don Draper watches quietly. Picture his crisp suit, his relaxed posture — leaning back, though still in control — and his steady gaze. Drink in his authority. When he speaks, his words are absolute, his voice steady, no matter how much he's had to drink, so sure of itself it's hypnotizing. "You've done well," the voice says, and approval saturates the room. See the glass of scotch as he holds it out and studies it, as if in it lies the secret recipe for his success. Draper is a sipping man; there will be no chugging, shooting, or downing in this office. These sips presuppose abundance: there will always be more scotch, more money, more beautiful women. They will continue to come and go and come again as if this life is certain.

Unlike Draper, I imagine that for my dad, drinking presupposes an uncertain life and is a ritual that calms and steadies him. As an artist who was thrust into a high-powered working world at an early age, my dad was always drawn to the kinds of drinking that slow the world down, that require the delicacy of a refined palate. Yet for my dad and Draper — the real man and the fictional — the glass, the peaty single malt, the warm wood of the bar or the private space of an office are materials with which they carve a powerful masculinity.

A Man Walks into a Bar

Strike that. A *woman* walks into a bar. She sits at the end, orders a Macallan twelve year, and takes out a book. "What are you reading?" The speaker is not an attractive man. The hem of his wrinkled shirt peeks out from behind his waistband; his pants bunch and bag around the knees; his shoes seem to sigh as he walks; and he wears an ever-so-slight sweat mustache on this hot, summer day. He is the kind of man who would never approach a woman like her.

But in this hothouse of masculinity, this man is no longer bound to himself. A few Buds in, and his wrinkled shirt no longer says "unkempt," it says "carefree"; his shoes don't sigh, they saunter; and his sweat mustache? Tangible evidence of his uncontainable virility. A couple more Buds and he knows, just knows, that the woman at the end of the bar wants him. The book is merely a decoy, of course, a thin mask behind which her aloneness says, "Take me."

When Peggy, Don Draper's secretary, earns a promotion to copy writer, Don offers her a glass of scotch. With her first sip, Peggy becomes the only woman in the agency to rise above secretarial status and enter the boys' club. Peggy also gets an office, with her very own door to close. In Draper's boys' club, and the contemporary one I seek entrance to, being alone means working, thinking, or creating. In this land of the free, heroes are made in private. They emerge from smoldering embers, morph from nuclear accidents, traverse great divides, battle entire armies with only a gun and a snide one-liner, then gather in bars where they drink to each other's health, pat each other on the back, and say, "You the man!" and "Dude, she wants you."

Though I might be sitting *at* the bar, though I might be drinking scotch, though I might be fearless and alone, I certainly am not *inside* the bar. Being inside means owning the space and having access to the blank slate–ness, that all-American dream of self-creation that a bar allows its male patrons such as the one who approached me. It is clear in these early years of drinking that the scotch, the bar, and my expert nose will not offer me the same passage to manhood as my male counterparts have. Instead, I am the blank slate, the white space of the all-American male's fantasy female, the conquering of whom and the terrain upon which his manhood is built.

Sipping is not enough.

Baptism by Broccoli

To be on the inside of the bar, to enter this magical realm of manhood and devil-may-care bravado, I sought whatever entrances I could. Although I might not, for example, come off as mysterious and intimidating sitting at the bar alone, I could down shots with the best of them. I mastered the after-shot poker face; no matter how bad the liquor, no curled lip or shiver here, no way, no how—I didn't even need limes or salt to throw it back. Real men, after all, know how to steel themselves against fire and learn to like it.

And what better way into the secret order, the internal architecture of the bar, than through its sewer system? If I had been the outsider before, felt exiled by the trappings of gender, surely I was close now, hugging the toilet seat and not even bothered by the stench, this being a dive bar and all. For what was more *inside* than a toilet, which opens itself to man and woman equally—your tired, your hungry, your poor. I marveled at the new me being born—surely stronger, more fearless (if not also dizzier, and it would help, too, if someone could please hold my hair?) as I arched and moaned over the portal to that other world, watching as whole pieces of broccoli poured forth—*That's strange*, I thought, *I could have sworn I chewed that on the way down*, but who was I to question the mysterious power of rum or the miracles of transformation, and what is sacrificed for the new? Out with the old (in this case, a delightful dinner of sautéed broccoli, brown rice, and tofu—great for keeping a girlish figure) and in with the new. Surely, surely, I was close now.

Bathroom Blow Jobs

There will be setbacks, of course. The toilet paper dispenser at eye level, the physical contortions required of you in such a small space. The wetness underfoot that you would rather not think about but you keep slipping, so there's no way around it. What some might call difficult, or inconvenient, or gross, you know is really character-building. Isn't this what your ancestors had in mind when they passed down their legacy of endurance? This family doesn't let mere physical obstacles break them. Each trouble is a test, every mountain an opportunity to climb and conquer. The phone-booth-size stall will be overcome; the aching knees will be weathered; the overwhelming circumference of this man's manhood will be surmounted; and you will triumph. For in the end, it's the size of one's suffering, the span of one's endurance, that determines greatness.

The Clothes Maketh (Not) the Man

I am a bartender now. I have left my academic job, PhD in hand, to live against the grain and pursue the great American dream. I am the lone cowboy, conqueror of wild territories, fierce galloper into the unknown. If I cannot conquer the terrain of the bar as a drinker, I will *be* the bar. I am the guardian of liquor, defender of freedom and honor and all other abstractions that can rouse even the drunkest of the drunk into battle, stumbling and slurring as they may be.

But the great American hero is not born overnight. And so I understand that I must start small — or, in this case, exceptionally large, as at my bar, The All-American (a super chain), everything is oversized and clad in picnic-basket reds and whites, including me. No matter that I'm wearing a child's short-sleeved shirt and baseball cap, or that my size ten orthopedic Mary Janes extend far beyond the hem of my black Dickies, or that I am encouraged to wear flair to "pep up" my presentation of self, I have made it, finally, into the heart of America. Here I've discovered cheese fries as large as a Californian desert; bacon-wrapped, jumbo shrimp atop onion rings *and* French fries; and bottomless glasses filled with eight different well liquors and twelve varieties of sucrose. While the world outside the bar might be difficult — promotions might be withheld, coveted houses remain out of reach, unpaid bills accumulate — The All-American offers comfort and possibility and the option, for an additional $2.99, to supersize. Your manhood might be questioned out there, but in here, you can be the man you want to be and more. It is my job to aid you in your self-creation via fried foods and booze. To the beat of Lady Gaga, to the buzz of The All American Frozen Booberry Martini, this land is your land. Have at it.

Argia

I have quit the All-American and taken another job as a bartender/cocktail waitress at a chain hotel bar that has me "Yes sir-ing" myself into a tizzy. "Don't say 'I don't know,'" they tell us, "Say, 'I'm happy to find out!'" "Don't say, 'Sure' or 'Yup,' say, 'Absolutely!'" "We're a team," they say, "a family! We want you to have room to be yourself, just no tattoos, jewelry, flashy hair, or makeup that stands out." In my oversized blue button-down shirt and black vest—a sad substitute for the crisp, ironed suit of Draper's profession—I represent an alluring combination of faux sophistication, servitude, and female acquiescence that comforts weary businessmen and assures them that, though they may not make more than $47 K a year (if they did, they certainly wouldn't be at *this* hotel), on the road, they are kings. Their Michelob ULTRAS will be ice-cold; the head on their eight-dollar Guinnesses will be moderate; and their every complaint (of which there are many) will be met with a smile. "Yes, sir; right away, sir . . ."

To make sure of it, there are cameras strategically placed to watch "the family" and keep us in line. As I skirt between bar and table, table and kitchen, I feel the camera burning into the secret self I harbor beneath the smiling serving girl. "Yes, sir; right away, sir . . ." Yet when I finally see the video stream one late night in the security office, I see only surfaces, an aerial view, servers and drinkers scattered like cattle across the room.

In the middle of a long, breakless shift, I disappear to a bathroom stall, beyond the reach of cameras, to devour boiled egg halves to sustain me. But protein can't satiate my hunger. The thing I thought would feed me—this myth of masculinity—only starves me further. Even the men out there—ye weary travelers—are starving. They down drink after drink and reach out toward the smiling serving girl, the lone hero really just lonely.

I have entered the boys' club and found it to be a deserted city. "It's down below there," I was told. It's at the bar, it's in the drink, it's in the swagger, it's in the heavy load you carry.

Remember the box that Don Draper's long-lost brother, whom he was not happy to see, left for him? In it were pictures of a poor, dirty boy, at the mercy of others. The box contained the child-hood that threatened to crumble the tower of manhood Draper had worked so hard to build. The same markers of manhood that made him also trapped him, like ice on a lake. The alive man, the vulnerable man who needs air and movement and flexibility to breathe — there he is, clawing at the surface, looking for a crack to break open and bust out of. We might drink to hide the cracks, but scotch or beer or whiskey or my current drink of choice, te-quila — those devilish imps — will also, in due time, be the very force that makes us face them.

That man, the mysterious and intimidating one at the end of the bar? Whom once upon a time I wanted to be? He just threw up outside. It may not have been broccoli, and it may or may not have been reconstituted whole, but tonight, he was me. The me I was when I was trying to be him. And that man with the sweat mustache, whose shoes sigh and shirt hangs? Sure, his beer's got him all worked up and playing the cocky dude, but when the woman he approaches turns him down, he's the same insecure boy he's been all his life. And my dad, the real man, my great American hero? His masculinity came at a great cost — the art-ist-him shut down while he did the things a man must do: work long hours, do everything himself as a lone hero must, and put his dreams of being an artist on hold. Only now, in his sixties, when he, too, sees something of the fiction that held him in sway all those years, does he talk of tending to the artist-him again.

When Peggy gets her own office, she also gets her own girl, to whom she can speak firmly and authoritatively. "Enough, Lola," she says when her secretary carries on about the cute new British guy. Lola tries to appeal to Peggy's sense of female solidarity: "You know there's something about the way he talks; I could listen to him read the phone book." But Peggy is firm. "Well when he gets to s," she replies, "I need Howard Sullivan at Lever Brothers," and then she walks briskly back into her office. Who does Peggy become in the privacy of her office and the public space of the agency? Peggy has been given the opportunity to drink scotch, make decisions, direct her own secretary; she is permitted to walk the men's walk and talk the men's talk. In other words, she can emulate the men around her. But emulation, I have learned, is not self-creation. Drinking like a sailor and emptying out my insides over a dive bar toilet, surprisingly, maketh not a man of me. Turns out, it maketh not a man of men either.

Behind Every Man Lies a Great Woman

Not long after quitting Hotel Bar, I land a job at a local cantina, where service isn't about serving, and where I don't have to play out someone else's idea of the female. I'm not here to seek entrance to the boys' club anymore. And in this bar, I'm not expected to help build men. I build drinks.

Grab a handful of mint leaves; feel them snap; smell the fresh zing! Drop them into a glass; top with lime, then the smallest squeeze of simple syrup. Wrap palm around smooth muddle; grind the wooden edge; feel the arm muscle flex and pulse; feel the mint and lime give. Break them down and from their essence, build. Add ice, rum, soda, lime, straw. Behold! This thing you made with precision and care and strength.

At the cantina, I master feats of great skill and coordination. I learn to hold three or more beer bottles in my arms while popping off their caps in one swift move. I learn to muddle five drinks at once, lifting the metal tin above my head and shaking the shit out of each drink. I move back and forth between brain and brawn, counting, surveying, assessing, then releasing myself into making. And I learn from the other bartenders how to stand my ground, how to make space for myself behind the bar while working harmoniously with others, how to be female and sexy without feigning availability, how to say no, and how to embrace the spilled drink, the broken glass, the mess of making.

Wear the sticky scent of citrus; plunge your hands into soapy water; drip juice from fresh strawberries onto the bar. Throw yourself into the working muscles: drag, heave, hoist, lift, snap; shake, stir, pour.

I learn from the work how to enter my body, my female body, not the one being looked at and written upon, but the one I discover is strong and agile, with muscles working to their limit — building, making, working, creating.

At the end of the shift, I sit at the bar; it's my turn. I made my drink myself — muddled basil and Rosangel's hibiscus tequila with lime and soda — and I sip it as I think about what I've accomplished tonight and all that has brought me to this drink. I've moved from sipping to downing to making, and now I'm back to sipping, but out of care, not imitation. I'm not drinking to become someone else; I'm not drinking to intimidate or impress; I'm not searching for a portal to an inaccessible city; I'm savoring the self I'm creating. And I'm letting my tired body unwind. This pause at the end of the night's work brings recognition of my own vulnerability, the mess I make in building this self, and the human inclination to reach beyond, to simplify, and to want. I understand that I've been part of the club of searchers and strivers and failures all along.

But I also know that failure is necessary for creation. My dad taught me that. Accidents, he's said about the creative process, are opportunities.

It's not in the ability to lift heavy objects or hold my drink or suck a man bone dry where I find my strength; it's in the soft lens of recognition, in the turning toward my own fumbling self and softening, not trying to hide her. And it's in the fluidity of self, the being able to let go of what holds us back, like myths, like what we thought was magic but was really accident, and continue to rewrite ourselves.

And so from the center of a deserted city, I say to myself: I see you, I forgive you, I admire you—you who have been tired, hungry, and poor. You who have journeyed from bar to bar, bathroom to bathroom, service job to service job to find your American dream. You weathered the flirtations of unattractive men; you endured compromising positions in the name of all that is reckless and holy; you left your comfortable academic job to wear embarrassing uniforms and be the bearer of cheese fries; you have drunk too much, and you will no doubt drink too much again; and you are, frankly, one of the best women I know.

gina barreca

▼ Permission Slips

*P*ermission slips
me a drink
almost imperceptibly
across the bar's top.

I sip and won't stop
until I slip, lose my
step, misspeak, mutter
then utterly permit no more
to pass my lips.

I'll slip out
unnoticed, no note,
not loud, yet
allowed

Down the hall
out the door

slip away

Leaving laughter behind me
on a sure footing,
no heel broken,
no slip showing

as per my mission.

▼ Moms' Club

The New Happy Hour

Recipe: The Momtini

Prep time: 20 minutes (2 minutes to pour, 18 to drink)

Mix equal parts friends, fun, and your favorite alcoholic beverage.

Serve immediately and, if possible, without children.

When we exchange our Prada bags for BabyBjörns, we also unwittingly check off the box that says "mothers don't drink." But just because we popped out a baby does not mean we still don't want to pop the Veuve Clicquot!

Why is it that as soon as we become mothers, we are expected to leave our cosmos at the bar and settle for reruns of *Sex and the City*? Are all mothers who crave a glass or two of wine regarded as closet alcoholics like Stefanie Wilder-Taylor[1] or Meg Ryan in *When a Man Loves a Woman*?

When I was single and living in New York City, I regularly went out for a drink with the girls. I loved these evenings (or Saturday afternoons or Sunday brunches) — they were a fabulous mix of fun, laughter, and group therapy with smart, funny, like-minded women. After I married and moved to Providence, Rhode Island, I continued the tradition with new friends, sharing a glass of wine with a gal pal after work or on the weekends in my new city. My friends and I always referred to these nights as "going out for drinks" or "cocktails with the girls."

1. See Jan Hoffman, "A Heroine of Cocktail Moms Sobers Up," *New York Times*, August 14, 2009.

So you can imagine my surprise when, after having my twins, the happy hour invites stopped and were suddenly replaced by e-mails and e-vites for Moms' Book Club, Mommy Spa Day, Make Your Own Purse Night, Mother of Twins Club, and—well, you get the idea. In my sleep-deprived, housebound-new-mommy state of mind (did I mention that I was socially starved after weeks of pink and blue onesies?), I dusted off my English major literary prowess and drove to suburbia to my first Moms' Book Club.

Once there, I quickly learned that you cannot judge a book club by its cover. When I arrived at my first "meeting," instead of the provocative book discussion I had expected, I was greeted with a formal wine tasting, followed by a gourmet dinner and after-dinner drinks that lasted well past midnight—on a week-night! And then the same thing began to happen again and again: Make Your Own Purse night offered pitchers of sangria, Mother of Twins Club was drinks and appetizers at a local pub, Mommy Spa Day featured mini-spa treatments accompanied by perfectly chilled Pinot Grigio and finger food at the country club. Soon I saw a trend in all these mommy events—they were our respectable, socially acceptable alibis for drinking. This got me thinking (and talking) about the strange double standard between the non-moms and the new moms. *What to Expect When You're Expecting* didn't have a chapter titled: "Top 10 Cute Ways for New Mothers to Secretly Steal a Cocktail." What happened to just saying (or even shouting) "I need a drink!"?

As I talked with other moms about this (over an Irish coffee during Knitting Club, of course), a common thread emerged: even when they try to hide it, all mothers (single or married, first-time or veteran) regularly celebrate, relax, and—yes—escape with a cocktail, all in the spirit of being a better mommy. A glass of Pinot Noir, or a chocolate martini or a pomegranate margarita—the cocktail does not matter, but the escape and the ability to temporarily blur reality does. Once, on a plane ride back from Las Vegas, another mother told me in a hushed voice that her nightly cocktail was her "mother's little helper," filling that time we all call the witching hour (just after the children's dinner and before Daddy returns home). The more I talked about this to friends and relatives, the more confessions I heard. One mom always jokes, "it's 5:00 p.m. somewhere" while pouring a glass of Chardonnay and calling her sister for a virtual drink date. Others have a weekly or monthly Moms' Club meeting that is *never* canceled. More attend Moms' Shopping Nights that involve strolling along quaint New England streets where each boutique offers sips of their favorite libations (one store owner and mother told me that these shopping nights can turn into shoplifting nights if the ladies get too tipsy).

Sitting at the computer with a glass of my favorite port, I have a realization: we really aren't any different than our single sisters. Sure, we are moms now. Okay, we left the city for the suburbs. Yes, we have children. Yes, some of us drive minivans, and many of us now call happy hours "moms' nights." But we will never pack away the Prada. We still have shrines to our Jimmy Choos. We will never, ever don mom jeans or need a TLC makeover. Regardless of labels and outdated stereotypes, we will always love and crave our cocktails with the girls. We are still as complicated and delicious as the perfect martini.

As I finish my drink before heading out to the Go Green Trunk Show at a nearby mom's house, I think that maybe I'll host the next event: a cocktail party.

▼ The Park Slope Stroller Wars

*I*n the leafy, tree-lined neighborhood of Park Slope, a Brooklyn area known for its historic brownstones, socialist-style food coop, highly rated public schools, and child-obsessed parents, the stroller moms (and dads) like to have a cocktail at the bar every now and again with their kids in tow.

Even Smartmom, a local blogger and newspaper columnist, liked to meet friends for a cosmopolitan while her daughter, the Oh So Feisty One (OSFO), slept in her stroller. Come to think of it, she remembers breast-feeding her toddler at the Second Street Café while sipping a glass of white wine.

But not everyone in this idyllic—and sometimes contentious—neighborhood likes to imbibe alongside moms and kids. Some find it annoying. Others find it inappropriate. Still others are convinced that the mothers are abdicating their maternal responsibilities.

So herein lies the tale of what happened when the owner of Union Hall, a local bocce bar popular with hipsters, rockers, and parents, decided to ban the Bugaboo set.

Once upon a time, in the winter of 2008, a group we'll call the Union Hall Mommy Group was in the habit of meeting one afternoon a week—when the bar was quite empty—in the 5,000-square-foot space. A converted warehouse with fireplaces, firesides, two indoor bocce courts, outdoor garden seating, and a downstairs bar and music venue, the space was more than big enough for a group of approximately ten mothers and their children.

Indeed, Union Hall, with its stately library décor and real

books on the shelves was an appealing space for the Union Hall Mommy Group. The bocce court added a recreational touch, and the fireplaces created a warm and fuzzy mood on a dark, wintry afternoon.

Ah, yes: winter in Brooklyn. Smartmom knows from her long-ago stint as a stay-at-home-mom (SAHM) that it's a tough season to be home alone with the kids. From November through March, many a Brooklyn day is too cold to enjoy the magnificent playgrounds of Prospect Park or to stroll up and down Seventh Avenue, the neighborhood's main shopping artery, in the hopes of running into a friend. And there are just so many classes (cooking for two-year-olds, sign language, and music for aardvarks) that you can afford to sign up for to get through the winter months.

Consequently, winter means a lot of time indoors, and moms and kids are likely to feel cooped up in their small, overheated Park Slope apartments.

Tick tock, tick tock.

Smartmom can well remember time standing still while she tried to fill the day with child-centric activities.

Sure, she loved being home with OSFO. But it was exhausting and sometimes downright boring. As OSFO grew from newborn to toddler, Smartmom felt pressure to play with her as much as possible (as she had been brainwashed by popular child development studies about the importance of brain development in children before the age of three). Even when she was bone tired and longed for a nap, even when a truly compelling issue of the *New Yorker* beckoned, Smartmom pushed herself to be the kind of mom who played with Teletubbies on the floor and made make-believe breakfast at the make-believe stove. She felt guilty when she wanted to check her e-mail or do some writing at her computer in the dining room. But OSFO took care of that: she learned early on how to turn the computer off.

Eventually, Smartmom discovered that in order to get some work done, she could put OSFO in the kitchen sink, where she loved to play with small plastic bowls in a soapy bath.

Still, Smartmom recognized that OSFO couldn't spend all her waking hours in the kitchen sink (much as OSFO would have liked to). That's why Smartmom organized a mommy group, not unlike the Union Hall Mommy Group, for camaraderie and support. An important social network, those groups are also an effective way to combat winter's cabin fever.

The trouble is that finding an adequate (and inexpensive) space for these gatherings can be a challenge. Smartmom's mommy group met at her apartment on Thursday mornings at 10:00. But sometimes the group was too big for the living room. And baby OSFO didn't much like sharing her Uglydolls with a bunch of unruly kids.

Smartmom can well understand why Union Hall was a great option for the Union Hall Mommy Group in 2008. Although Smartmom and OSFO, who was eleven that year, had aged out of the whole mommy group thing, Smartmom followed the story closely. The moms could buy bar snacks like French fries, mini-hamburgers, and sandwiches for a politically—and nutrition-ally—incorrect supper for their spawn, and they could also order drinks—alcoholic or not—for themselves. Perfection.

Members of the group assumed that Union Hall would be happy to have them there. Wasn't their business welcome the off-peak hours? Wasn't the place practically empty before happy hour at 5:00 p.m.?

So not only were the moms and kids having fun at Union Hall, they actually believed they were helping a local business out.

But as the saying has it, no good deed goes unpunished.

At first the bar welcomed the group, which met for a few months before there were any signs of trouble. The moms would set up in the area near the bar, where there are upholstered chairs and small tables. They'd order drinks and food and get a chance to schmooze and booze while their kids played together or slept in their strollers.

But then, suddenly, Jim Carden, the owner of Union Hall, had a change of heart. He went from being a fairy godmother for these stroller moms to a wicked witch. It all happened very suddenly. One day, the mommy group showed up at Union Hall for their usual sit and sip, and there was a sign on the front window: "No Strollers Allowed."

Members of the Union Hall Mommy Group were stunned.

It wasn't like anything bad had happened. There had been no incident or accident. No furniture broken or barware savaged. Undoubtedly the group left behind a bit of a mess — a trail of Cheerios, perhaps, or a spill or two from a sippy cup. But the moms always tried to clean up after themselves, and they always left a generous tip for the bartender and the wait staff.

The "No Stroller" sign went up without an explanation, and the moms were upset. Not only did they have nowhere to go on winter afternoons now, but they felt like they were being singled out, segregated personae non gratae in their neighborhood bar.

Well, don't think this didn't cause an immediate brouhaha in a neighborhood rife with local bloggers and national journalists. When word got out about the "No Strollers" policy at Union Hall, Carden was simultaneously under fire and hailed as a drinking-class hero for putting it up.

Even Smartmom got in on the act and wrote a fairly even-handed article for the *Brooklyn Paper* and her blog, *Only the Blog Knows Brooklyn* (OTBKB). She was later interviewed on National Public Radio about the situation, and subsequently there were articles in the *New York Times*, the *Daily News*, *Time Out*, and other media outlets about this maelstrom in a martini glass.

As you can imagine, members of the Union Hall Mommy Group took to the blogs to slam Carden. One mom who lived in what she describes as a "650-square-foot apartment, where there's barely enough room for her, her husband, their 18-month-old and an elderly, deaf cat" wrote to Smartmom to say that she was very unhappy about this turn of events.

"In the winter, sometimes we go to a bar during 'off' hours with our kids, let them run around, let the adults chat and have a drink whether it be alcoholic or not," she wrote.

But many childless locals defended Union Hall's policy. In fact, those who were against moms in bars were the most vocal on local blogs. The incident seemed to unleash an untapped torrent of negativity toward mothers and kids.

"I went to Union Hall [and] was appalled to be sitting next to toddlers while trying to talk to my girlfriend (sometimes graphically) about life," wrote one poster on *Brooklynian*, a local blog. "So I've not been back. I'll give it another try if it's not going to feel like a preschool."

And that was one of the more polite posts!

On Smartmom's blog, the comments (mostly anonymous) were more vitriolic:

"These stupid yuppie idiot parents make me sick. CHILDREN DO NOT BELONG IN A BAR! What part of that do you people not get? If being inside with children is making you all 'stir crazy' then you should have thought of that BEFORE you had the damn kids! As a non-parent I do NOT want to go into a bar and see children, I don't give a crap how well behaved they are," wrote one commenter on OTBKB.

Parents from an older generation found fault with the moms who insisted on bringing their kids to Union Hall; not surprisingly, the E-word ("entitlement") was summoned.

"Bringing children into the bar . . . another example of the entitlement of the 'new' Park Slope parents. It's all about them. I have already raised my kids and have earned the right to go into an adult environment without having to have toddlers run around," wrote another commenter on OTBKB.

Others were annoyed that bars were being used as a meeting place for children's play groups: "Bars are for adults not for children. Having a child does not make you special or entitled to rights—bring your child to the bar when he/she turns 21."

Still others felt that if women wanted to drink when they were with their children, they should do it somewhere other than in public. In other words, mothers should not be seen or heard when they're drinking.

"Why would anyone want to take their children to a bar? If they want to meet up with other mommies and their children and have a drink, why can't they host their friends at their house where their children are welcome?" wrote one angry commenter.

Some viewed the presence of a mommy group at a bar as an assault on other patrons, who didn't want to be around children: "Who wants to hear some annoying baby when they just want to have a beer? Some parents really need to grow up. Either get a nanny or babysitter or don't have kids at all!"

Peter Loffredo, a local psychologist and blogger, saw the issue through a larger psychological lens. In a comment on OTBKB, he delineated the two types of narcissism, "primary narcissism" and "phallic narcissism," that develop during childhood. The first appears in the first year or two of life, the second at age three or four. He wrote:

> In the first case, the child never learns to accept that he is not the center of other people's universes. In the second type, the child becomes addicted to attention and adoration. In both cases, the child develops a fragile, dependent personality.
>
> Both types of narcissism stem from having parents who are overly involved with the child in inappropriate ways. Does taking a child to a bar constitute inappropriate?

Clearly, that "No Strollers" sign really touched a nerve. Many people wondered if there was something wrong with this generation of parents, who seemed unable to cut the umbilical cord and go out alone. The level of nastiness in the comments attested to the barely concealed bitterness that exists between parents and nonparents, and even between parents who have different approaches to child rearing.

And it really seemed to bring out the venom in childless locals, who were sick and tired of the fact that no place was off limits to the stroller set.

Smartmom knew that Carden certainly wasn't the first bar owner in the neighborhood to lower the boom on the Bugaboo set. There was actually a historical precedent. Who can forget the bartender at Patio, a bar on Fifth Avenue in Park Slope, who wrote the now-famous (or infamous) "Stroller Manifesto"?

"What is it with people bringing their kids into bars?" wrote the bartender, Andy Heidel, in thick white chalk back in August 2006. "A bar is a place for adults to kick back and relax. How can you do that with a toddler running around?"

The message was scrawled on an A-frame blackboard that Heidel placed on the sidewalk outside the bar, where it drew a lot of attention. From there, his "manifesto" made the rounds of the blogosphere and national media, igniting a fiery debate.

Smartmom could understand both sides. Yes, it's convenient to bring your kid with you if you don't have a baby sitter. But do parents really need their Brooklyn Lager with a side of Brooklyn babies?

After a few weeks, the Union Hall imbroglio died down, and Carden finally admitted in an interview with Smartmom in the *Brooklyn Paper* that putting up the "No Strollers" sign without an explanation to the neighborhood had been a big mistake. Indeed, it was insulting to the moms, who had done nothing wrong. And it was a public relations nightmare for Carden, who was being portrayed as antichild by the media.

"It was strictly about liability," Carden said. "A lot of parents are great and mindful. But some are not that attentive to their kids when they're in here. This is a bar with an open stairwell and a bocce court. This is a business, and we don't have the staff to police it."

Was Carden suggesting that some of the moms were neglecting their maternal duties while drinking in his bar? It is possible, Smartmom supposes, that the moms were too involved in their conversations — and their Chardonnay — to notice that their kid was running relays on the bocce court or slamming into waitresses carrying food to the tables.

But Smartmom can relate to that. Her threshold for mayhem was so high when OSFO was a noisy toddler that she found that she could carry on long conversations with friends while her daughter was screaming, crying, or otherwise causing public havoc.

Sometimes she needed the adult conversation that much.

Still, Smartmom seriously doubts the babes and toddlers at Union Hall were any more out of control than a bunch of twenty-one-year-olds after a few drinks.

In an interview, Carden assured Smartmom that Union Hall had nothing against the Union Hall Mommy Group. Far from it. Indeed, that would be sacrilege (and bad business) in a family-focused neighborhood like Park Slope. And Carden and a few of the bar's employees have kids of their own.

"But Union Hall is not a community center," he continued. "We want to be here for a long time. We've got a long lease. We don't want to jeopardize that for anything [with a possible lawsuit]."

So after strollers were barred from Union Hall, where did the Union Hall Mommy Group go? It was early February when the "No Strollers" sign appeared, and there were still quite a few weeks before March came in like a lion and went out like a lamb. Smartmom thinks they probably migrated to Park Slope's Community Bookstore, with its fancifully decorated—but small—children's room in the back, complete with a live lizard named Gomez. Or perhaps they chose the Brooklyn Public Library or the Brooklyn Museum. But it wasn't the same. You can't exactly order a drink in the children's room of the library.

Sadly, Smartmom knew that the moms would have to face the fact that Park Slope is not a small village in the English countryside, with a charming pub that doubles as a gathering place for families with children and dogs. Smartmom loved the feeling of those places back in 1978 when she took a bicycle tour through southern England.

Indeed, Union Hall is a grown-up bar. Smartmom would even go so far to say that it is designed as a place for the younger Park Slope crowd. Smartmom and her husband, Hepcat, were like that once, and they used to hang out at a funky bar they nick-named "Windows on the Weird" on Avenue A, in Manhattan's Lower East Side.

Interestingly, Smartmom can't remember seeing any kids at Windows on the Weird or any of the other Manhattan bars (Puffy's, El Teddy's, the Ear Inn, the Great Jones Café) that they frequented when they were young and childless in the 1980s. Things were different then. Kids existed, of course, but they didn't have the elaborate social lives they do today. And the parents didn't feel entitled to introduce them to the adult world at such a young age.

Clearly, Park Slope's single and childless "young people" need a place to hang out, just like Hepcat did when he had a specially designated bar stool at the Great Jones Café. But parents and kids also need places to go that aren't Disney-esque play spaces or smelly, indoor playgrounds.

So that's the tale — and the conundrum — of what happened in the leafy, contentious, and not always mom- and child-friendly neighborhood of Park Slope when the owner of a popular bar put up a "No Strollers" sign and caused quite a stir.

But there's more. Without the help of a Prince Charming or pack of dwarves, Carden changed his mind and reversed his policy. He publicly apologized for posting the sign without an explanation and announced that on one or two designated afternoons a week, he would once again welcome moms and kids for some down time and drinks at the bar.

It was a positively fairy-tale ending and a victory for the Union Hall Mommy Group, who went back to their meetings at the bar with their kids.

Flash forward to 2010. The babies and toddlers of the Union Hall Mommy Group are probably in kindergarten or elementary school now. Their moms don't need a mother's group anymore, and they've all moved on to other things.

But although time marches on, there are always young moms and children to take their place. Parents seem quite comfortable bringing their children just about everywhere in and around Park Slope. But that doesn't mean that people don't complain: the issue of kids at bars still seems to agitate some in the neighborhood.

In October 2010, Daryl Lang wrote a scathing post in his blog, *History Erase Button*, about why he's leaving Park Slope for lower Manhattan: "By now, it's old news that Park Slope parents take their kids everywhere. On any given night, you'll find young children in the bars with their moms and dads. Walk around after midnight and you see parents out with kids in strollers or on trikes and scooters. I love kids, but I get a little weirded out when I see a toddler in a bar: I guess I can't cuss here."

While the issue of kids in bars hasn't exactly gone away, the neighborhood hasn't seen a major meltdown since 2008. Perhaps the Union Hall incident was a watershed moment in the movement to include babies and children in nearly all adult activities. Indeed, the Union Hall Mommy Group pioneered a trend that is now accepted—whether enthusiastically or grudgingly—by members of this community.

Surely it was a victory for those who bristle at the separation of parents, children, and those without children.

And it was a victory for those who oppose the demonization of women when they choose to have a drink at the end of a long day with their kids.

Finally, it was victory for those who, like Smartmom, abhor the idea that women are required to become some "holier than thou" version of themselves when they become mothers. Nine months of pregnancy and a baby doesn't mean you suddenly stop wanting to socialize or sip spirits from a glass.

▼ One Not-So-Simple Question

i grew up in suburban New Jersey in the 1970s, and like so many of us who turned eighteen when that was the legal drinking age, my life is replete with drunken, drooling exploits. Before I hit that magic age of drinking and voting, I often lied to my parents about my whereabouts, took the 82 bus across the George Washington Bridge, the A train downtown, and repeatedly flourished a fake ID made from my mother's discarded driver's license. I was in a sickening stupor the night my ex-boyfriend, the famous brewer, asked me out. I spent a night reassembling furniture and sponging up blood after a Lithuanian guy arrived at my high-school best friend's party with a machete and a bad attitude. There were too many tequila shots in Baton Rouge. Too much vodka in Venezuela. A lot of stumbling down Manhattan sidewalks.

But I figured a book about women and alcohol would be bursting with uproarious or wrenching drinking tales, told through the hazy dual lenses of liquor and time, so instead, I e-mailed a simple question to a dozen girlfriends.

"Why do you drink?" I asked.

I thought I'd get a few clever, animated stories. Some zesty anecdotes. A couple of quips, a few dark responses.

My friend Claudia texted me: "Because my mother-in-law's visiting." She doesn't have a mother-in-law. But she knows mine.

As it turned out, the question wasn't so simple.

"I drank for different reasons at different points in life. All congruent to Erikson's psychosocial stages of development," my friend Annie, a reflective therapist, wrote from her Blackberry.

I raised my eyebrows. The eight stages include hope, will, purpose, and love — all issues that could drive a person to drink.

Uh-oh, I thought. This isn't the stuff of swizzle sticks and pint glasses.

"To make it through stressful family holidays, dull anxiety, and because I can," wrote Michele, who is, by her own definition, an "annoyed suburban mom and former party girl."

To be honest, I've never given much thought to why I drink. Certainly because it's social, and I like the fuzzy hum at the end of the day provided by a gimlet or a glass of wine. A *mojito* or a beer. Because in high school, peppermint schnapps made our cheap pot taste like Doublemint gum. It made mistakes feel like good choices, even back then.

Alcohol is a flexible substance; it provides many things for many people. My friend Louise, who is a funny, zany, hip young grandmother, wrote: "Alcohol is the most effective agent in calming my restless soul. But as I look back over decades of this behavior and assess the timing, I recognize another reason I drink. To drown my sorrows."

My foolishness was in thinking the replies I'd get to my question would be quick and glib because my friends and I tend to be quick and glib. But most of us have a complex relationship to alcohol. It feels good (until it feels bad), and many of us have alcoholics in our lives. We don't want our kids to drink until they can make responsible decisions. So it's a risk to write an essay about embracing the social, enjoyable, nonmoralistic side of drinking. But that's part of drinking, too: it's fun.

As the replies to my not-so-simple query rolled in, I kept hearing: "Good question. I never thought about it, I just do it." An unanticipated level of thoughtlessness in a bunch of women, all college educated, a few with PhDs, who haven't done much without conscious thought in twenty years.

But maybe that's also the joy of drinking for those of us who can actually do it "casually." There is so little we do without thinking these days. We perform our jobs thoughtfully; we listen to our partners patiently (generally); we give our kids the attention they need. We move through our lives sensibly. As a result, I feel a little guilty making my friends reflect on one of the few things they do with little consideration as to why. I fear my question made them overanalyze something they don't really ever think about.

For me, drinking makes meeting people easier, and (before I was married, both times) sleeping with them easier, too. People get funnier, or at least they think they do, until they get stupider. It's the only legal drug other than pharmaceuticals, and I'm no longer willing to get arrested. I want to be a reasonably good role model for my son.

Back in the days when my friends and I were younger (and drinking was still a statement), we believed we were drinking with abandon. We danced on bar tops, sipped rum out of half empty Coke cans at the beach, spent too much time in clubs. But there was probably an element of intent. We were giving some nonexistent entity the finger, showing other people who didn't care that we were able to step over the line of propriety and still wake up the next morning and go to work.

In this age of responsibility, in a culture that finds sin in so many places, perhaps we should, at least occasionally, see a relaxing, chilled cocktail or two — or a few glasses of wine — as just that and nothing more. Extend a little permissiveness to ourselves, and if we don't have a drinking problem, leave motive out of the martini glass.

There are so many things my friends and I used to do casually and without deep thought, some of them safer than others. We all had a freedom in our lives that barely exists anymore. The loosening of daily ties that alcohol offers may be a small doorway back to our more libertine past, a way to laugh a little longer, let go a little easier, still feel like bad girls, and maybe that's not so terrible. Maybe I can retract my question. And at least sometimes, we can sip our way through the moral conundrum of "why we drink," and just enjoy.

Contributors

gina barreca, who lives in Connecticut, grew up in Brooklyn and on Long Island. She is the author of eight books, including *Babes in Boyland: A Personal History of Coeducation in the Ivy League*, and *It's Not That I'm Bitter — or How I Learned to Stop Worrying about Visible Panty Lines and Conquered the World*. She is a professor of modern British literature and feminist theory at the University of Connecticut, and you can read more of her work at www.ginabarreca.com. At a party, you would probably find Gina holding forth. If she's lucky, she's also holding a glass of Perrier-Jouët, mostly because she thinks the bottle is fancy.

amy bloom hails from the home of Long Island iced tea but now lives in Connecticut. She is the University Writer-in-Residence at Wesleyan University and owns a bottle of sherry. She is the author of two novels, three collections of short stories, and a book of essays.

kerri brown is a recent graduate of the University of Connecticut. While there, she spent as much time as she could writing, possibly more time working on various nonfiction, poetry, and fiction pieces than studying for any of her other classes. She'd like to toast her fabulous feminist professors for showing her that writing about women can be fun. When she's at a party, you will see her unable to let go of her college youth, casually pouring herself a glass from a bag of Franzia or sipping a chilled Keystone (Light).

nicole callihan writes poems, stories, and essays. Her work has appeared in *Cream City Review*, *L Magazine*, and *Painted Bride Quarterly*. She teaches at New York University and in schools and hospitals throughout the city. A founding member of the Brooklyn Writers Collective, she was named a Rockefeller House Fellow. Nights, she returns to Brooklyn to be with her family and pour herself a big glass of cold white wine.

susan campbell is an award-winning columnist at the *Hartford Courant* and the author of *Dating Jesus: A Story of Fundamentalism, Feminism, and the American Girl*, a Connecticut Book Award finalist. You can read more of her work at www.datingjesus.net.

rita ciresi (www.ritaciresi.com) is the author of five works of fiction, including the novels *Pink Slip* and *Remind Me Again Why I Married You*, and the linked short-story collection *Sometimes I Dream in Italian*. She is a professor of English at the University of South Florida. Her drink of choice is tap water.

catherine conant lives in Berlin, Connecticut, and teaches, performs, and coaches the art of oral storytelling in nonprofit settings. Her work has been published in *40 Fathers*, *My Little Red Book*, and *Who Killed June Cleever?* You can hear her stories on her CDs, *Exit 11 and Other Stories* and *Far From Perfect*. She believes that one day she will own a decent set of both red and white wineglasses.

louise crawford, who lives in Brooklyn, writes the Smartmom column for the *Brooklyn Paper*. She runs *Only the Blog Knows Brooklyn* (www.otbkb.com) and the *Brooklyn Blogfest*. A writer of fiction, she has written for the Associated Press and Newsweek.com. You can find Louise at Bar Reis drinking Sailor Jerry rum.

niamh cunningham, who lives in New Haven (but prefers New York), is the author of the blog *A New York Minute*. It has tens of readers. An editorial assistant at Yale University Press, she hasn't published much yet, but she enjoys receiving rejection letters written to "Mr. Cunningham." You can read her work at www.31stavenue.wordpress.com. At a party, you'll find Niamh holding a glass of Pinot Grigio. If the wine is warm, she's clearly spent too much time talking, so remind her to drink up.

sarah deming is the author of the novel *Iris, Messenger*, about the Greek gods in suburbia, for ages 9 to 109. She also ghostwrites erotic novels. Before becoming an author, Sarah was a Golden Gloves boxing champion, chef, and yoga teacher. She lives in Brooklyn but drinks Manhattans.

kristen dombek's essays can be found in *n + 1*, *The Painted Bride Quarterly*, and *TDR: The Drama Review*. She teaches in the Princeton Writing Program and drinks in Brooklyn.

liza donnelly is a staff cartoonist at the *New Yorker* and the editor of *Funny Ladies: The New Yorker's Greatest Women Cartoonists and Their Cartoons*, in which she chronicles the history of women in *New Yorker* cartoons both as illustrators and as subjects, and *Sex & Sensibility*, cartoons from ten female cartoonists exploring the female perspective on love and sex. With her husband, Michael Maslin, she wrote *Cartoon Marriage: Adventures in Love and Matrimony by The New Yorker's Cartooning Couple*. She is also a public speaker and has spoken for TED (Technology, Entertainment, Design). Liza is on the faculty at Vassar College. At a party, you'll find she's holding a glass of red wine.

jill eisenstadt is the author of the novels *From Rockaway* and *Kiss Out* and the coauthor and producer of the feature film *The Limbo Room*. Her shorter work has appeared or been anthologized in the *New York Times*, *New York Magazine*, *Vogue*, *Elle*, *Bomb*, *Queens Noir*, and *Best American Sex Writing 2008*, among other places. Jill teaches at Eugene Lang College, in the New School in New York City.

laurie fendrich, a professor of fine arts at Hofstra University, is an abstract painter who lives and works in trendy Tribeca. Her art was recently the subject of a retrospective museum exhibition whose catalog contained a witheringly unnegative essay by the Pulitzer Prize–winning art critic Mark Stevens. She has published many essays on the role of art and artists in society in order to ensure that she's disliked by an appropriate number of people in the art world. Her Monday dinners consist of dry-roasted peanuts and Sancerre.

nicole hollander lives in Chicago. Her new book is *The Sylvia Chronicles: 30 Years of Graphic Misbehavior from Reagan to Obama*. She is a Lillet fancier, and if she can't get that she will take a beer with a shot of Jameson on the side.

stephanie k. hopkins left the ivory tower to become a full-time writer and bartender. She lives in New York and is currently working on a collaborative memoir about her bartending adventures. She is a founding member of the Brooklyn Writers Collaborative. Her work has appeared in such journals as *Painted Bride Quarterly* and *Blithe House Quarterly*, and she can muddle a *mojito* faster than you can say, "Make mine a double!"

beth jones lives outside Boston and is the coauthor of *Three Wishes: A True Story of Good Friends, Crushing Heartbreak, and Astonishing Luck on Our Way to Love and Motherhood*. She's written for the *New York Times*, the *Boston Globe*, *Marie Claire*, and numerous other publications. She climbs ice in the winter and rides a bike with cleats. She didn't get a tattoo until she was thirty-six. Find out more (including that gimlets are her drink of choice) at www.Beth-Jones.com.

pamela katz is a screenwriter and novelist who lives in Brooklyn, writes about Germans, teaches in the graduate film program at New York University's Tisch School of the Arts, and does her best drinking (and eating) in France. Her credits include: *Rosenstrasse, The Other Woman, Divorce on Wheels,* and *Remembrance.* She is a frequent collaborator with the director Margarethe von Trotta; their latest work is *The Controversy,* a dramatic film about Hannah Arendt. On a hot summer evening, Pam enjoys a cold glass of French rosé. Katz is currently writing a forthcoming book about the tempestuous partnership of Kurt Weill and Bertolt Brecht (creators of *The Three-penny Opera*).

lindsey keefe, who lives in Charlottesville, Virginia, received her BA from the University of Connecticut and her MA from elsewhere. She wrangles XML by day and blogs at soppho.com, which even her mother does not read. If ever you give her a business card at a party, Lindsey will gladly accept it as a coaster for her gin and tonic.

wendy liebman (www.wendyliebman.com) has been doing stand-up comedy for more than half her life. She's been seen on Letterman, Leno, and Carson (Johnny, not Daly), has had specials on HBO and Comedy Central, and is in the documentaries *The Aristocrats* and *The Boys: The Sherman Brothers' Story.* She lives in Los Angeles with her saintly husband, amazing stepsons, and overfed dogs.

ami lynch is a vice president at a public health and research and evaluation firm, and debates with herself about whether she wants to one day be a tenured professor. She defended her dissertation while eight months pregnant and received her PhD in public policy in 2006, focusing on gender policy. She researches hate crime and gender-based violence. She is married, has a precocious toddler who challenges her to "make mine a double" every day, and lives in Arlington, Virginia.

dawn lundy martin is the award-winning author of two books of poetry: *A Gathering of Matter/A Matter of Gathering* (2007) and *DISCIPLINE* (2011). She is a member of the avant-garde poetry and performance trio, The Black Took Collective. She also writes essays and can be found, when she is not writing, either teaching at the University of Pittsburgh or drinking a perfectly crafted vodka martini, a tad dirty with Spanish olives.

maggie mitchell is a professor of English at the University of West Georgia, where she teaches nineteenth-century literature, creative writing, and film studies and edits *LIT: Literature Interpretation Theory*. Her short stories have appeared in the *Southern Indiana Review*, *Saranac Review*, *American Literary Review*, *Green Mountains Review*, and *Blueline*. She has also published scholarly articles on nineteenth- and twentieth-century British fiction. At a party you might find her in a corner, surveying the room while sipping a glass of wine.

sarah rasher hails from Chicago but lives in Connecticut, where she is a doctoral student at the University of Connecticut. Sarah has published in *The Chronicle of Higher Education* and is writing her dissertation on queer studies in Renaissance drama. At a party, you'd find Sarah holding her girlfriend's hand and a vodka tonic with an extra lime wedge.

karen renner teaches classes in American literature at Northern Arizona University. Her dissertation, a study of deviant figures in antebellum literature, contains a chapter devoted to drunks but — not surprisingly — very few of the texts she looks at are about women, and certainly none is celebratory. Her current work is on "evil" children in film and literature, which she hopes will point her to more promising company. Aside from admitting to a predilection for bright colors, she couldn't tell you her favorite cocktail, and that's the way she's gonna keep it.

sophia romero was born and raised in Manila, the Philippines. She is the author of *Always Hiding*, a novel about illegal immigration. She also writes a blog called *Shiksa from Manila*, based on the imaginary life (some say it's autobiographical) of Amapola Gold, a Filipino woman married to a Jew from Queens, as she romps through life as one half of an interfaith, intercultural marriage. Sophia lives in Brooklyn and, when sober, is usually in the company of her husband, two children, and Roxy, a kerry blue terrier.

greta scheibel spent two years in a beautiful village in the southern highlands of Tanzania. There, as an environmental extension agent, she taught beekeeping, animal husbandry, and winemaking. Currently, Greta lives in exotic Dar es Salaam, TZ, where she is the Executive Director of United Planet Tanzania. You can read more

about the adventures of Greta Scheibel at www.aisforadult.blogspot
.com. Whether at home in New England or out traveling the world,
she enjoys finding the little adventures in each day, always with a recognizable drink in hand.

laura rossi totten has handled book publicity campaigns for ce-
lebrities and bestselling authors for two decades. Her career has included work at some of New York's top publishing houses — including
Random House, Bantam Doubleday Dell, Dial Press, Viking Penguin,
and W. W. Norton — as well as at an award-winning Boston public relations firm. She now runs her own PR agency. At a party, you'll find
Laura sipping Veuve Clicquot.

fay weldon, CBE, lives in Dorset, England. She is an essayist, play-
wright, journalist, and novelist. Her international bestsellers include
The Life and Loves of a She-Devil, *Down among the Women*, *She May Not
Leave*, and *Chalcot Crescent*. A professor of creative writing at Brunel
University in West London, Fay can often be found holding a glass of
Dom Pérignon or a Diet Pepsi, but not both at once.

Jacket illustration by Liza Donnelly

Website: http://whendotheyservethewine.com/

Blog: http://lizadonnelly.com/

Library of Congress Cataloging-in-Publication Data

Make mine a double: why women like us like to
drink* (*or not) / edited by Gina Barreca.

p. cm.

ISBN 978-1-58465-759-0 (cloth: alk. paper)—
ISBN 978-1-61168-213-7 (e-book)

1. Women—Alcohol use. 2. Drinking of alcoholic
beverages—Social aspects. 3. Drinking of alcoholic
beverages—Psychological aspects. I. Barreca,
Regina.

HV5137.M35   2011

362.292'1—dc23   2011017940